DIMEBAG

Written and edited by Susan Doll and David Morrow.
Designed by Lisa Wright/redbird visual communications

Copyright © 2008 by the Estate of Darrell Abbott.
All rights reserved. No part of this publication may be
reproduced, stored, or transmitted by any means in any
medium without written permission from the copyright
holder.

ISBN: 978-0-9818827-0-3

10 9 8 7 6 5 4 3 2 1

CONTENTS

INTRODUCTION
Dime Shines

The life and times of Dimebag Darrell Abbott is more than a tale of a heavy metal god with killer musical instincts who was gone before his time. It's the story of a kid from Arlington, Texas, whose talent for the guitar was so monumental it transcended any musical genre; it's the story of a hard-partying rock star who never let fame eclipse his sweet nature and gentle soul; and it's the story of a passionate musician who inspired, and continues to inspire, new generations of guitar slingers.

In these pages, the real Dime shines through in the dozens of rare family photos, stunning portraits by today's biggest rock photographers, and the words of those who knew him best—his family, friends, and the musicians who admired and respected him. You'll travel alongside a legendary rock hero as he grows from a typical suburban kid to a teenage guitar phenomenon to one of the most talented and most beloved heavy metal icons the world has ever seen.

ONE OF THE MOST INFLUENTIAL STYLISTS
IN MODERN METAL, DIME HAD THE GIFT
OF THE RIFF.

LEFT: DIME COULD BE AN OUTRAGEOUS PARTY ANIMAL OFFSTAGE, BUT ONSTAGE, HE WAS A SERIOUS MUSICIAN. HERE, HE MESMERIZES THE CROWD AT MILWAUKEE'S SUMMERFEST IN 2004. ABOVE: AT THE HISTORIC MONSTERS OF ROCK CONCERT IN MOSCOW, DARRELL GREETS THE MILLIONS OF RUSSIAN FANS WHO WERE EXPERIENCING HARD-CORE METAL LIVE FOR THE FIRST TIME.

DARRELL'S CAREER WAS DOWNRIGHT INCENDIARY IN
2004 AFTER FORMING A NEW BAND, DAMAGEPLAN,
WITH HIS BROTHER VINNIE. LEFT: DIME ROCKS
CHICAGO'S HOUSE OF BLUES IN NOVEMBER 2004.
THIS PAGE: EARLIER THAT YEAR, HE THRILLED A
HOMETOWN AUDIENCE AT THE FREAKERS' BALL AT
THE SMIRNOFF AMPHITHEATER IN DALLAS.

DARRELL HAD A SPECIAL CONNECTION TO DEAN GUITARS MOST OF HIS LIFE. IN 2004, HE INKED A DEAL WITH DEAN THAT RESULTED IN A LINE OF GUITARS SPECIALLY DESIGNED AND DECORATED WITH DIME IN MIND, INCLUDING THE DIME-O-FLAGE (THIS PAGE) AND THE FBD TRIBUTE ML (RIGHT).

DIME EARNED HIS STATUS AS A
LEGEND NOT ONLY THROUGH HIS
MAGNETIC STAGE PRESENCE BUT ALSO
THROUGH HIS LARGER-THAN-LIFE
PERSONALITY. BOTH CAME NATURAL
TO HIM SO HIS PERFORMANCES AND
HIS INTERACTIONS WITH FANS WERE
ALWAYS WARM, GENUINE, AND REAL.

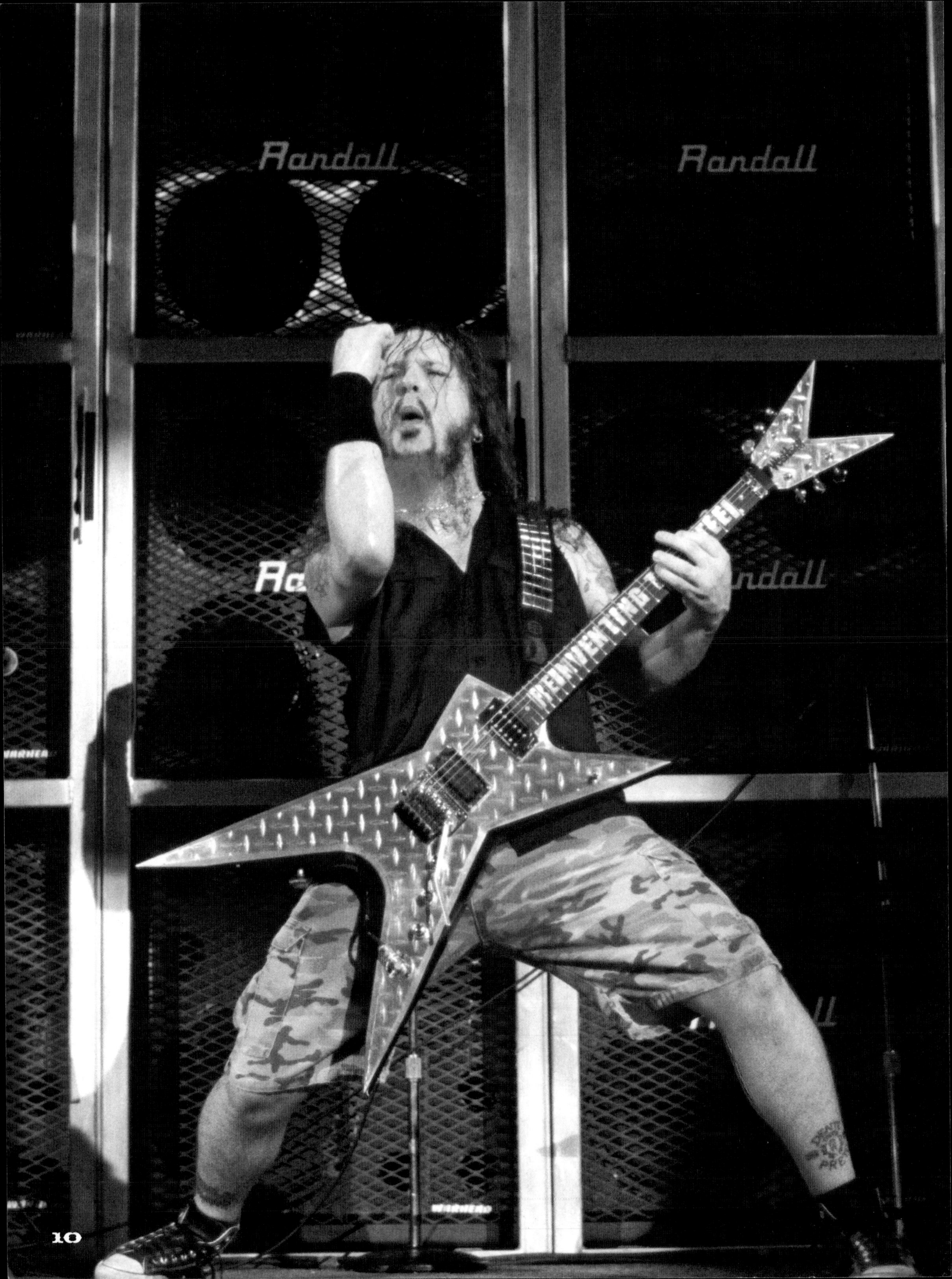
Randall
Randall
REINVENTING

DIMEBAG DARRELL ABBOTT (1966–2004) WILL BE REMEMBERED AS A PREDATOR IN THE ARENA OF METAL AND REVERED FOR HIS LEGENDARY GUITAR SOLOS THAT WERE RELENTLESS AND UNCOMPROMISING. THIS IS HIS STORY . . .

A MUSICAL FAMILY

BLOODLINE

imebag Darrell Abbott—heavy metal guitar god, purple-bearded party animal, and genuine freethinker—did not hail from zany L.A. or gritty New York City. He was born in Arlington, Texas, a small community of ordinary folk looking to escape the hustle and bustle of Dallas and Fort Worth. With a small-town vibe and a suburban appearance, Arlington is an all-American town. After Pantera became famous and Dimebag notorious, both Darrell and his bandmate and brother Vinnie chose to remain in Arlington—hometown boys through and through.

The sons of Jerry and Carolyn Abbott, the brothers grew up in a typical loving family, with parents who supported their interests and nurtured their talents. As kids they had the same interests as other boys their age. Vinnie was into sports and for a time oceanography, while Darrell raced through Arlington on his skateboards and bicycles. Darrell and Vinnie's interest and passion for heavy metal—a type of music that flaunts society's rules and pushes its boundaries—was not an act of rebellion against their childhood. It was an act of artistic expression that grew out of the love and support they experienced while growing up.

CHAPTER 2

THE ABBOTTS OF ARLINGTON—
VINCE, JERRY, CAROLYN, AND DARRELL—
ENJOY A MERRY CHRISTMAS.

THE ABBOTT BROTHERS WERE TWO YEARS APART IN AGE. IN THIS 1970 PORTRAIT, VINCE (LEFT) IS ABOUT SIX, AND DARRELL (RIGHT) IS FOUR.

Darrell and Vinnie were not only close in age but also close in spirit. They naturally gravitated toward the same pastimes—from riding bikes and skate boards to building models to eventually playing music. Once they both became interested in music, they felt a hunger to be the best they could be.

"[VINNIE'S] THE MOST AMAZING BEST FRIEND I COULD EVER HAVE."

—DARRELL QUOTED BY PATRICK DOUGLAS, GREAT FALLS TRIBUNE, DECEMBER 10, 2004

The boys' musical interests were piqued after the Abbott family moved into their own newly built house on Monterrey Avenue in Arlington. One night, Jerry came home after work about 2:30 in the morning and stumbled over a strange-looking suitcase in the hallway. As soon as he got up the next day, he made a point of asking about the mystery case by the front door. Carolyn responded that Vinnie had tried out for the school band, and his teacher had assigned him to the tuba. "Tuba, my ass!" exclaimed Jerry, a guitar player in country and rock bands, "Not in my family." Jerry suggested that Vinnie ask his music teacher if he could play the snare drum, and much to Jerry's relief, the teacher agreed. In an interview in *Guitar World* magazine, Vinnie recalled that he had actually awakened his dad one morning by practicing the tuba, which alerted Jerry to the new instrument in the house. Whatever the sequence of events, Vinnie's career as a tuba player was extremely short-lived.

At first, both Vinnie and Darrell played the drums, but the older brother grew considerably better, partly due to the instruction he was getting in the school band. Rock legends Alex and Eddie Van Halen had also both started as drummers, and when Alex became better than Eddie, the former wouldn't let his little brother play anymore; similarly, when Vinnie realized he was better than Darrell, he didn't want to relinquish his drums to his kid brother. So, Darrell turned to a new instrument.

One day when Jerry was sitting at the kitchen table restringing his guitar, Darrell asked him for a special present for his twelfth birthday. "Dad...is there any chance I could get a guitar?" Already

DARRELL (BELOW) AND VINNIE ENJOYED AN ALL-AMERICAN CHILDHOOD IN A COMFORTABLE HOME IN THE QUIET COMMUNITY OF ARLINGTON.

enamored with Ace Frehley of KISS, he had decided he wanted to be a guitar slinger. Jerry took him to a music store in Fort Worth, and the two perused the inventory. Some guitars looked right but didn't sound good; others sounded right but didn't feel good. He passed on the Fenders, and he didn't care for the Gretsch design. Finally, he settled on a copy of a Gibson Les Paul made by the Hohner Guitar Company. Later, when Darrell was a teenager and an accomplished guitarist, he turned to Dean Guitars, beginning a lifelong love affair with their instruments and designs. But in the beginning, the Hohner Les Paul copy turned out to be the perfect choice.

At home, Darrell endlessly stood in front of his mirror and posed with the guitar—sometimes in full KISS makeup. Vinnie used to pass by his room and notice him playing air guitar. One day he joked, "Dude, are you ever going to learn to play that thing."

Vinnie didn't realize it, but he had thrown down a gauntlet to Darrell, who eagerly picked it up. A short time later, Darrell knocked on Vinnie's door and said, "Hey man, wanna jam?" Vinnie was skeptical at first, but when Darrell broke into Deep Purple's

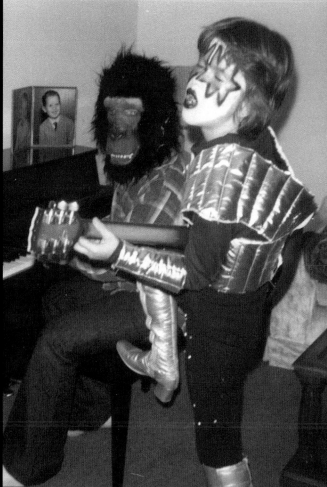

VINNIE AND DARRELL JAM IN COSTUME. DARRELL HOLDS HIS FIRST GUITAR, A HOHNER LES PAUL COPY, WHILE CHANNELING HIS HERO, ACE FREHLEY OF KISS. DARRELL AND HIS MOTHER MADE HIS OUTFIT TOGETHER.

1972 classic "Smoke on the Water," he joined in. By this time, Vinnie had added six toms to his drum set plus a double-kick bass, so the sound was hard and heavy. The pair played the famous opening riff for several hours—until the police came and asked them to stop.

Darrell learned to play from listening to his favorite records and bands, and then emulating the riffs and solos on his own. He also sought out Jerry, who taught him the basic chords behind the sounds he heard on his records. In addition, Jerry showed him how to listen to a song and dissect what the guitar player was doing. After a few months of these unique lessons, Darrell was able to figure out the guitar parts on his own.

Though always close, Darrell and Vinnie became inseparable from this point onward. At ages 12 and 14, respectively, the brothers were motivated by their love for music and fueled by their love for each other. The pair practiced in their garage daily. They set up their own rigid rehearsal schedule in which they played music together two hours a day no matter what. Other aspects of their lives, such as school, simply came second.

After the brothers had rehearsed together for about a year, their first attempt at a rock group came together. It began when Vinnie fell in with a couple boys from the school band at Bowie High School, including Tommy Bradford, the drum major with the marching band, who played bass guitar, and Terry Glaze, who played keyboards and guitar. Tommy and Terry wanted Vinnie to help them start a band, but Vinnie said he wouldn't join without his brother. Terry and Tommy didn't want a kid in the band—after all, Darrell was an adolescent in braces stuck in the purgatory of junior high school—but Vinnie held firm. They finally relented, and a very young Darrell Lance Abbott joined the band. Many years later and many miles down the road, Dimebag Darrell would return this favor to his brother in a profound way.

"IT WAS ALWAYS A NONSTOP HUNGER TO GET BETTER, TO LEARN MORE...WE DID THIS TOGETHER...."

—VINNIE PAUL, INTERVIEW, JULY 2007

The first official performance by the band was sponsored by the German class at Bowie High School. About 400 enthusiastic kids attended, and the boys got a taste of their future—or at least most of them did.

As it happened, Tommy Bradford left the group early in the game, and another member of the school band, Rex Brown, took his place. Vinnie and Rex had met in jazz-band, and the two had hit it off. During band practice at school, they would sometimes break into "2112," the well-known song by Rush, which always landed them into trouble with the band director. Vinnie knew that when Rex's name cropped up to replace Tommy, he would definitely

YOUNG, EAGER, AND HOPEFUL: THE EARLIEST INCARNATION OF THE BAND CONSISTED OF TOMMY BRADFORD (LEFT), TERRY GLAZE, DARRELL, AND VINNIE.

be trouble. Rex smoked, drank beer, and was always late for class, but he was an outstanding bass player. He played with a pick, which gave more definition and percussion to his sound than Bradford, who had played with his fingers. Everyone was excited to bring Rex into the group, and Vinnie relented, but he laid down some rules for practice: No smoking in the house and no drinking. At his very first practice in Vinnie and Darrell's garage, Rex brought cigarettes and a six pack of beer. Vinnie thought for certain that the band would fall to pieces. However, as soon as the four boys started jamming together, they clicked. It was their sound that pulled the four young musicians together into the band that would be known to the world as Pantera.

Over the next few months, the four practiced together in the Abbott garage and later at a local skating rink. Every so often, the police stopped by and issued a ticket for "disturbing the peace"—an appropriate metaphor for the impact the Abbotts would come to have on the world of popular music.

QUIT YOUR DAY JOB

VINNIE AND DIME BOTH HELD JOBS AS TEENAGERS, BUT NOT FOR LONG. MUSIC WAS ALL THAT MATTERED TO THE BOYS, AND THEY JUST COULDN'T SEE THEMSELVES DOING ANYTHING ELSE.

VINNIE SPENT A SHORT TIME WORKING FOR FOTOMAT, A NATIONAL CHAIN THAT SOLD FILM AND OFFERED PHOTO DEVELOPING FROM SMALL BOOTHS SET UP IN SHOPPING MALL PARKING LOTS. THE EXTRA MONEY WAS NICE FOR A WHILE, BUT THE JOB PROVED TO BE A DISTRACTION FROM HIS PURSUIT OF MUSIC.

DARRELL WORKED FOR A FAST-FOOD RESTAURANT CALLED CAPTAIN DEE'S—FOR THREE DAYS. IT DIDN'T TAKE HIM LONG TO REALIZE THAT HE JUST WASN'T CUT OUT FOR REGULAR WORK. THIS WAS THE ONE AND ONLY JOB HE EVER HELD. OTHER THAN THIS BRIEF STINT, EVERY NICKEL HE EVER EARNED CAME FROM PLAYING THE GUITAR.

Decades before Dime and Vinnie, another pair of Abbott brothers teamed up on the guitar and drums. This photo from the 1940s shows Darrell's grandfather, L. T. (Lonnie Trozy) Abbott, behind the drum kit and his great uncle Ace (front left), who played rhythm guitar. Their West Texas band, the Rhythm Kings, specialized in popular Western Swing tunes of the day. L. T. also sang and played guitar and piano.

Let's All Go to the Hi-Ho

JERRY Abbott began his lifelong relationship with music when he started taking **PIANO LESSONS** at age eight. Like so many American teenagers in the 1950s, he became fascinated with the music of **ELVIS** Presley and **JERRY LEE** Lewis and began **PRACTICING** their songs on his own, becoming good enough to play at **SCHOOL PARTIES** in pick-up bands with his friends. One of those friends, Mack Dumas, contacted Jerry several years later and asked him to **JOIN** the band he was in, Tooter Boatman and the Chaparrals, as piano player. Over the next decade, Jerry became a **SEASONED** club musician, playing the guitar and piano and singing in rock, country, and rhythm-and-blues bands at Texas **HOT SPOTS** with names like the Hollywood-a-Go-Go, the Ritz Starlight Room, and the Hi-Ho Ballroom. Jerry **MOVED** his family to Arlington after accepting a gig as part of the **HOUSE BAND** at the Hi-Ho, which is located in nearby Grand Prairie. Jerry's career gave Darrell and Vinnie their first **EXPOSURE** to music, and his **CONNECTIONS** to the local scene helped them get their band into the local clubs.

DAD ALWAYS USED TO TELL US,

"SON, YOU CAN BE A DOCTOR, OR A LAWYER, OR A MUSICIAN.

BUT IF YOU'RE GONNA BE A MUSICIAN, YOU'VE GOT TO BE

BETTER THAN EVERYBODY ELSE AND

DIFFERENT FROM EVERYBODY ELSE."

—VINNIE PAUL, ON HIS FATHER, JERRY, INTERVIEW, JULY 2007

THREE GENERATIONS OF THE
ABBOTT FAMILY TRACE THE
EVOLUTION OF POPULAR MUSIC
FROM COUNTRY TO ROCK 'N' ROLL
TO HEAVY METAL. FROM LEFT TO
RIGHT, VINNIE, L.T., JERRY, AND
DARRELL.

DARRELL ABBOTT HOLDS HIS
GRANDFATHER'S MARTIN D28.
EVEN AS YOUNG AS FIVE OR SIX,
HE SHOWED AN INTEREST IN THE
GUITAR; HE USED TO WATCH CLOSE-
LY WHEN HIS FATHER RESTRUNG
OR WORKED ON HIS INSTRUMENT,
AND HE WOULD LISTEN TO HIM
PRACTICE FOR HOURS ON END.

21

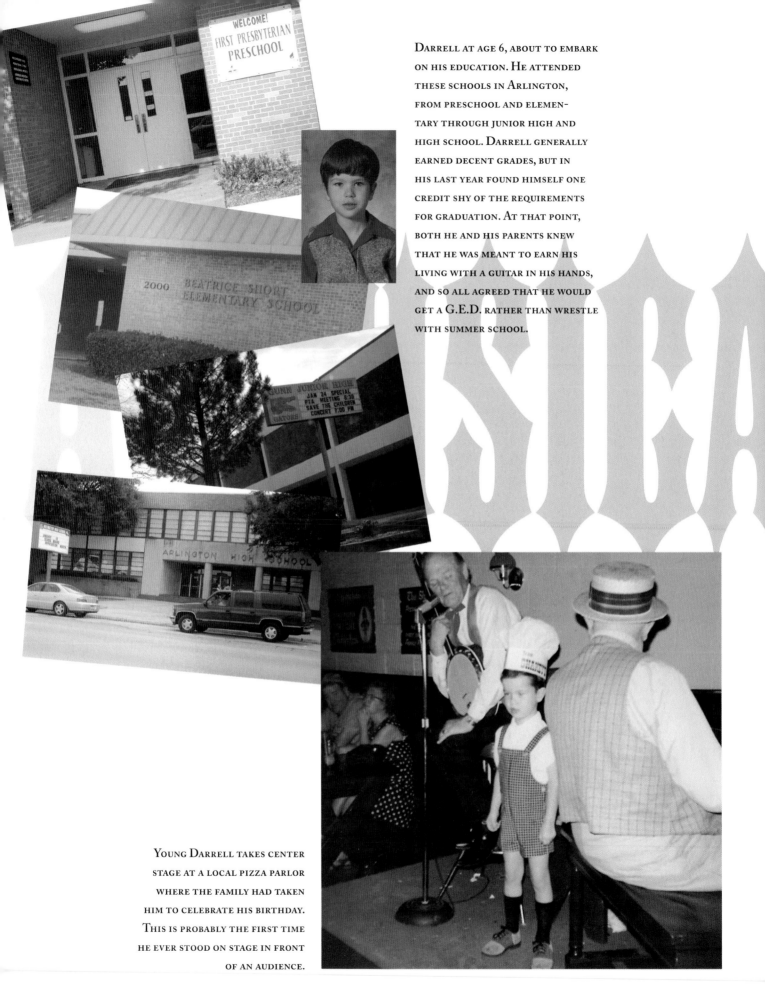

DARRELL AT AGE 6, ABOUT TO EMBARK ON HIS EDUCATION. HE ATTENDED THESE SCHOOLS IN ARLINGTON, FROM PRESCHOOL AND ELEMENTARY THROUGH JUNIOR HIGH AND HIGH SCHOOL. DARRELL GENERALLY EARNED DECENT GRADES, BUT IN HIS LAST YEAR FOUND HIMSELF ONE CREDIT SHY OF THE REQUIREMENTS FOR GRADUATION. AT THAT POINT, BOTH HE AND HIS PARENTS KNEW THAT HE WAS MEANT TO EARN HIS LIVING WITH A GUITAR IN HIS HANDS, AND SO ALL AGREED THAT HE WOULD GET A G.E.D. RATHER THAN WRESTLE WITH SUMMER SCHOOL.

YOUNG DARRELL TAKES CENTER STAGE AT A LOCAL PIZZA PARLOR WHERE THE FAMILY HAD TAKEN HIM TO CELEBRATE HIS BIRTHDAY. THIS IS PROBABLY THE FIRST TIME HE EVER STOOD ON STAGE IN FRONT OF AN AUDIENCE.

JERRY AND DARRELL POSE FOR
A SNAPSHOT AT JERRY'S HOUSE,
WHERE DIME RECEIVED HIS FIRST
INSTRUCTIONS IN THE ART OF
SHREDDING. NOTE JERRY'S DOBRO-
STYLE GUITAR LEANING AGAINST
THE SOFA TO THE LEFT,
INDICATING THAT GUITAR
LESSONS WERE IN PROGRESS.

In Jerry's Words
"A VanHalen Album in One Hand and His Guitar in the Other"

Thinking back 30 years, Jerry Abbott recalls how 11-year-old Darrell first began to exhibit a real interest in guitar playing. The story comes out like he's telling it for the hundredth time, and still his voice carries an unmistakable ring of pride.

"Darrell had ridden his bicycle over to my trailer house. I heard this **KNOCK** on the **DOOR**, and there he stood. He had a **VAN HALEN ALBUM** in one hand and his **GUITAR** in the other, and he said, 'Dad, I want you to **SHOW ME** how to play something off this record.' Well, I never had heard of Van Halen before, but I had a little old record player so we put it on and **STARTED LISTENING** to it. The song was called 'Runnin' with the Devil,' and the title alone scared me into next week. It took me a few minutes to figure out something that was in the ballpark at least, but I showed him certain **POSITIONS** that [Eddie Van Halen] was playing, and how they related to the **KEY** that the song was in, and stuff like that. He left there with a little bit of an **UNDER-STANDING** of it all, and it didn't take a whole lot of those **SESSIONS** until he was able to pick things out **ON HIS OWN** and work his way through them. He seemed to have a **NATURAL BENT** for picking up things he heard on records. So it was a **COMBINATON** of me relating the absolute **BASICS** of the instrument to him and of his own **DRIVE** to perfect it."

CAROLYN'S CORNER

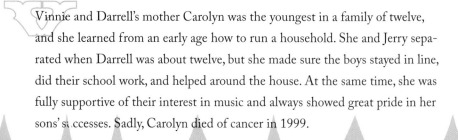

Vinnie and Darrell's mother Carolyn was the youngest in a family of twelve, and she learned from an early age how to run a household. She and Jerry separated when Darrell was about twelve, but she made sure the boys stayed in line, did their school work, and helped around the house. At the same time, she was fully supportive of their interest in music and always showed great pride in her sons' successes. Sadly, Carolyn died of cancer in 1999.

VINNIE AND DARRELL SHOW OFF THEIR CATCH WITH THEIR MOTHER CAROLYN AFTER A FAMILY FISHING TRIP.

IN THIS 1990 PHOTO TAKEN AT A CLUB CALLED THE BASEMENT, THE FAMILY RESEMBLANCE BETWEEN DARRELL AND HIS MOTHER IS OBVIOUS. NOT ONLY DID HE LOOK LIKE HER, BUT HE ALSO PICKED UP HER TALENT FOR MAKING EVERYONE FEEL AT EASE BY TREATING THEM LIKE A TRUE FRIEND.
INSET: CAROLYN AT AGE 17.

"WHETHER SHE WAS **BROKE** OR NOT, BETWEEN **HER** AND MY DAD, ONE WAY OR ANOTHER, **SHE MADE SURE** WE GOT WHAT WE NEEDED FOR **SCHOOL BAND**, OR **WE GOT** WHAT WE NEEDED FOR **INSTRUMENTS**, OR WHATEVER. SHE WAS **ALWAYS** OUR **BIGGEST FAN.**"

—VINNIE PAUL ON HIS MOTHER, CAROLYN, INTERVIEW, JULY 2007

DIME SHARES THE WEALTH WITH HIS MOM AT A CELEBRATION FOR HER BIRTHDAY AT NICK AND SAM'S STEAK HOUSE IN DALLAS, IN A SMALL WAY PAYING HER BACK FOR THE MANY YEARS OF LOVE AND SUPPORT.

CAROLYN SHOWS OFF A PAIR OF SLACKS SHE RECEIVED AS A BIRTHDAY GIFT FROM THE FAMILY IN THE EARLY YEARS.

I'm Your Biggest Fan

Darrell was fascinated with hard rock and heavy metal when he was growing up, and there were a great many bands that he loved with a passion. But one of his hands-down, no-holds-barred favorites was KISS. That may be no surprise, as the band was huge in the mid 1970s when Darrell was just beginning to discover popular music. It is remarkable, though, that Dime never gave up his devotion to the band, even after his own accomplishments took him to similar dizzying heights.

CAROLYN MADE DARRELL A KISS COSTUME ONE HALLOWEEN, AND AS A HARDCORE MEMBER OF THE KISS ARMY, HE NEVER TIRED OF WEARING IT. THE MAKEUP, OF COURSE, WAS THE TRADEMARK OF DARRELL'S FIRST GUITAR HERO, ACE FREHLEY. YEARS LATER, WHEN PANTERA OPENED FOR KISS IN ARGENTINA, DARRELL AND THE BAND DONNED KISS MAKEUP AFTER THE SHOW. STANDING WITH KISS MANAGER DOC MAGHEE, DARRELL STILL PROUDLY WEARS THE FREHLEY MAKEUP.

DARRELL PROUDLY SHOWS OFF HIS ACE FREHLEY T-SHIRT WHILE VISITING WITH JERRY.

When Dime bought his own house in Arlington, he made sure that Ace, Gene, Paul, and Peter would have a place in it. Mounted on the wall directly across from the front door, these four vibrant busts greet visitors as soon as they walk through the door.

A Few of Darrell's Favorite Bands

ANTHRAX
BLACK SABBATH
DEF LEPPARD
DIO
DOKKEN
GRIM REAPER
IRON MAIDEN
JUDAS PRIEST
KISS
KROKUS
METALLICA
MÖTLEY CRÜE
VAN HALEN

Dime wails on his Dean ML back in the early days in Arlington. Note the KISS belt buckle—his inspiration was never far away. Dime also sported an Ace Frehley tattoo on his chest. When he finally got to meet Ace, Dime asked him to sign the tattoo and then rushed out to have the signature inked.

LOCAL LEGEND
Grind That Axe!

CHAPTER 3

As though preordained to a path laid down for them long ago, Darrell and Vinnie were rock stars almost from the day they picked up their instruments. Most new bands struggle in the beginning to find their audience, but the newly formed Pantera—with Darrell and Vinnie at the core—attracted local supporters and fans early on. Friends volunteered to help them set up, and Darrell never had to carry his own gear as pals, pickers,

HANDS PUMPING IN THE AIR WITH A POWER THAT IS ALMOST PALPABLE, THE CROWD ENTHUSIASTICALLY RESPONDS TO THE MUSIC. DARRELL REELS BACK ON HIS HEELS, ABSORBING THEIR ENERGY AND SENDING IT BACK TENFOLD.

THOUGH STILL A TEENAGER, DARRELL EXUDES ALL THE CONFIDENCE AND COOL OF A BIG-TIME ROCK STAR.

and compatriots hustled to help the young guitar slinger. Though the boys never let the adulation go to their heads, it was clear they were going to be a local sensation.

Darrell and Vinnie's father, Jerry, had already begun to serve as their manager, working with them at Pantego Sound Studio, booking them into local clubs, driving them to shows, running sound during performances, and selling their merchandise between sets. With the two Abbott brothers anchoring the band, Jerry watching out for them as manager, mother Carolyn providing moral support, and close friends rounding out the band members, the success of the group was truly a family affair. In an era when conservative pundits were attacking rock music, particularly the heavier groups, as an affront to American traditions and virtues, the band bridged the seeming contradiction between family values and rock 'n' roll.

Through Jerry's connection with Pantego Sound, the Abbott brothers met Ricky Lynn Gregg, the popular lead singer of a local band called Savvy. Pantego Sound's second engineer, Jerry Hudson, ran sound for Gregg's band and also recorded them, so

Darrell and Vinnie were able to watch as the band worked through their songs in the studio. Gregg was a good showman who played lead guitar and sang in the same vein as Journey and Genesis. His musical abilities and his offstage honesty and sincerity were an influence on Darrell and Vinnie. He encouraged the boys and helped get them in to see their first live show at the club where he regularly played, which was also called Savvy's.

The boys began to pester Jerry about getting them a show at Savvy's. Eventually, the club owner agreed to let their band do an opening set, and a date was selected. The show, which featured danceable cover tunes and a couple of original songs, went off without a hitch and proved the perfect beginning for the young band. The boys' friends and families supported them as they appeared in a professional nightclub setting, and the group got a feel for the hard work that was part and parcel of playing music for a living.

The band members were still teenagers, with Darrell the youngest at 14, when the band began to play professionally. They focused on perfecting cover tunes enhanced by Darrell's increasingly

A very young Darrell rocks the crowd at a local nightclub.

Heavy metal, 1980s-style: Poodle perms, spandex, and torn tees.

adept guitar playing, generally starting their sets with well-known tunes that audiences could dance to, then moving into heavier material. They quickly gained a large, loyal following based on their reputation as the best cover band around, and more and more clubs booked them. Within, a few years of their Savvy's debut, the band was playing clubs throughout Texas that specialized in heavier rock music or heavy metal.

Influenced by KISS and dominated by glam rockers such as Ratt, Poison, and Mötley Crüe, the metal scene of the early 1980s was awash in young men with long, poodle-perm hair, brightly colored spandex pants, and ripped t-shirts and bandanas. Pantera followed suit, adopting the look though not necessarily the glam metal attitude. Serious about

their music and their careers, they were influenced more by Van Halen's musical abilities and showmanship than by Mötley Crüe's posturings.

"WE'RE FROM TEXAS.
WE'RE INDEPENDENT.
WE DO OUR OWN THING."

—VINNIE PAUL, 1996

Perhaps this was due to their roots, which reached deep into the heart of Texas. As Vinnie explains it, Texas has a "real vibe" because the "people are righteous towards each other." The state is renowned for its homegrown musical styles and stars, including the blues of Stevie Ray Vaughn, the outlaw country of Willie Nelson, and the hard-rocking boogie of ZZ Top. In addition to these big names, Texas sports a vibrant club scene of local-based performers who often enjoy large followings but lack the opportunity to attract a major record label.

As the boys tore through clubs like The Basement in Dallas, The Rock of Texas in Denison, Joe's Garage in Fort Worth, Circle in the Square in Shreveport, Louisiana, and the Village Inn in Texarkana, Darrell's vigorous solos added to his growing reputation as a local guitar legend. It became mandatory for the young slinger to launch into mammoth solos lasting as long as 30 minutes—giving the rest of the band time for a break. The boys attracted an extremely loyal fan base while playing the clubs, which served them well over the years, but the band—especially Darrell—became doggedly determined to land a record deal.

> "MY GOSH, I SAW THAT KID AND I WANTED TO GIVE UP," SAID ALAN PETSCHE, A GUITARIST WHO... FIRST SAW [DARRELL] PERFORM AT... THE LOFT. "HE WAS PROBABLY 14 YEARS OLD. IT WAS JUST UNNATURAL."
>
> —DALLAS-FORT WORTH STAR-TELEGRAM, DECEMBER 10, 2004

Jerry began recording the band at Pantego Sound whenever time allowed. The early sessions were loose, with the band members having fun while they got acquainted with the recording process and got past any nervousness about performing in a studio. As Terry Glaze recalled later in an interview for

Full in Bloom Music, "It was a great experience that helped me out so much in my later career. I wasn't intimidated by the "red" light when I got into other studios."

At first, Pantera recorded cover tunes as demos for club owners. However, Jerry offered them some advice very early on that would prove invaluable: Writing your own songs is a significant part of the music business, and in many ways, it is as important as a musician's performing abilities. With that in mind, Darrell and Vinnie began to develop their own songs, along with Terry Glaze.

The next logical step was for the band to release a record—something that could be played on the radio. Working with Jerry at Pantego, the boys refined their best original work into an album titled *Metal Magic*, a name taken from one of the main tracks. Jerry decided to also use "Metal Magic" as the name of the record label because he truly believed that's what the band created—metal magic. Released in 1983, when Darrell was barely 17, the album featured ten songs, including "Nothin' On But the Radio" and "Ride My Rocket," two odes to youthful lust that were in keeping with the hair-metal

THE COVER ART FOR THE BAND'S FIRST ALBUM, *METAL MAGIC*, WAS REPEATED ON THEIR BACKSTAGE PASSES.

genre so popular during that era.

The following year, the group released *Projects in the Jungle*, a far superior effort that covered a broad spectrum of metal. From "All Over Tonight" to "Like Fire," the songs had been honed to a professional

INSTEAD OF "DIAMONDS," DIAMOND DARRELL LANCE ACCESSORIZES IN CHAINS, SPIKED JEWELRY, AND PLENTY OF ATTITUDE.

level and were a stronger showcase for Dime's guitar riffs, though the lyrics still focused on love, sex, and rockin' hard. *Projects* was followed in 1985 with *I Am the Night*, a transitional album that revealed the band's path toward faster and harder metal, as evidenced by such cuts as "Down Below," "Valhalla," and "Right on the Edge." Darrell's guitar sounded crunchier, and his plentiful solos were more aggressive.

DARRELL "CUTS UP" IN THE STORAGE ROOM AT PANTEGO SOUND STUDIO.

All the while, the young rockers kept their eye on the goal of securing a major-label deal. Small labels, such as Mechanic Records, expressed interest, but Jerry and the band members were intent on holding out for a major name. In the meantime, the band began to pop up on the front covers of the influential heavy metal magazines, including *Crucible, Rock Hard, Kerrang, Metal Forces,* and *Heavy Metal Times*. In European underground and metal magazines, reviews of Pantera's albums could be found right next to those for Iron Maiden and Metallica.

At one point, Richard Bron of the British company Bronze Records came to Killeen, Texas, to see the boys tear up Woodstock, one of the many clubs on their Texas circuit. That night, Darrell pulled out all the stops and played a monster solo. Bron loved the band and the audience's reaction to them, but he felt that they were just too young at that time. When he told Rex, Terry, Vinnie, and Dime that he would not sign them, their faces couldn't hide their disappointment. Still, they picked themselves up and moved on.

Around 1986, Terry Glaze decided to leave the band for a group called Lord Tracy, which already had a major record deal. For several frustrating months, Vinnie, Darrell, and Rex tried hard to find

THIS PHOTO OF A 22-YEAR OLD DARRELL APPEARS ON THE INSIDE BOOKLET OF THE ALBUM *POWER METAL*, RELEASED IN 1988. DIME WAS READY FOR THE INTERNATIONAL FAME THAT WAS JUST AROUND THE CORNER.

a replacement for Glaze. Several likely—and not so likely—candidates auditioned and even played gigs with the band, but none had that metal magic. One day, Vinnie found himself on the phone with Phil Anselmo, the charismatic singer of the New Orleans band Razor White. He knew and loved all the same music that had inspired Pantera, and an instant bond was formed on his first visit to Texas. The gravel-voiced Anselmo, who could command a room with his presence, easily stepped into the role of lead singer. The new lineup of Rex, Darrell, Vinnie, and Phil released *Power Metal* in 1988. The album is often discussed as Phil's debut with the band, but it is also a magnificent showcase for Dime's guitar style at a transitional point. His solos on such tracks as "We'll Meet Again" are massive and include some signature Dimebag riffs, while his guitar work in "Power Metal" and "Over and Out" typifies the all-out shredding of speed and power metal.

But the question remains: How could the band have survived month after month with no regular frontman? Because the heart of the band was Darrell's phenomenal metal guitar and its soul was Vinnie's double-kick drumming. Innovative as musicians and inseparable as brothers, Darrell and Vinnie *were* destined for success.

In the beginning.... there was youth, drive, and ambition. The band members' tender age never worked against them; instead, it manifested itself as a potent energy that audiences found infectious.

Darrell and Vinnie saw Van Halen perform at the Cotton Bowl Stadium in the early 1980s, which influenced them to follow their dream. Not only did Darrell want to play like Eddie Van Halen, he and Vinnie found a kindred spirit in the way brothers Eddie and Alex Van Halen interacted onstage. According to Vinnie, "Dime loved Randy Rhoads and a lot of these other players, but Eddie was the guy...."

THE BAND CUT THEIR TEETH PLAYING PARTIES
AND CLUBS ALL OVER TEXAS, WITH DARRELL
GAINING A REPUTATION AS A GUITAR SLINGER
WHO COULD RIP THROUGH EXTENDED SOLOS.
AS THE CROWED COAXED HIM ON, HE WOULD
WALK OUT ONTO THE FLOOR WITH A SPOTLIGHT
FOLLOWING HIS EVERY STEP. HIS LONG HAIR
FLEW BEHIND HIM, AND HIS ARM BANDS AND
LEGGINGS FLAPPED IN THE BREEZE AS HE
SOLOED HIS WAY INTO THE HEARTS OF HIS
TEXAS FANS—WHO REMEMBER DARRELL TO
THIS DAY.

THE VERY FIRST PUBLIC-
ITY PHOTO INCLUDES THE
BAND'S ORIGINAL BASSIST,
TOMMY BRADFORD (LEFT),
WITH TERRY GLAZE,
DIME, AND VINNIE. BRAD-
FORD LEFT THE BAND,
PERHAPS UNDER PRESSURE
FROM HIS GIRLFRIEND,
WHO FELT THE MUSIC WAS
TAKING UP TOO MUCH OF
HIS TIME.

Personal Mgt: Jerry Abbott
2310 Raper Blvd.
Arlington, Tx. 76013
(817) 461-8481

PANTERA

Rockin' Through Texas

By the mid 1980s, Pantera had become a fixture at most of the rock clubs within 100 miles of Arlington: Cardis in Houston; Joe's Garage in Fort Worth; the Aragon Ballroom, Matley's, The Ritz, the Bronco Bowl, the Arcadia Theater, and The Basement in Dallas; The Ranch in Muenster; Woodstock in Killeen; Rock of Texas in Denison—the list goes on and on and on . . .

AS THE EXPLOSIVES WENT OFF AND THE SMOKE ROLLED, DARRELL WOULD SOMETIMES JUMP OFF THE SPEAKERS, BOUNDING ONTO THE STAGE IN A MOVE DESIGNED TO LIGHT UP THE CROWD.

THANKS TO LONGTIME FRIEND KENNY "PYRO" WEBSTER, THE BAND WAS ABLE TO INTEGRATE FAIRLY SOPHISTICATED LIGHTING AND PYROTECHNICS INTO THEIR EARLY SHOWS, SUCH AS THIS BARN-BURNER AT THE ROCK OF TEXAS IN DENISON, ABOUT 40 MILES NORTH OF DALLAS. WEBSTER EVEN COMBINED SOME HEAVY DUTY B-52 LANDING LIGHTS INTO THE USUAL CLUB LIGHTING TO ADD TO THE HIGH-VOLTAGE EFFECT.

THE NEW ROCK OF TEXAS PRESENTS

PANTERA

METAL MAGIC

IN CONCERT FRI & SAT OCT 14 & 15 $3⁰⁰ COV

DIME ROCKS HARD DURING A BEER-KEG REHEARSAL AT JOE'S GARAGE IN FORT WORTH. THE BOYS PLAYED THERE AT LEAST ONCE A MONTH BECAUSE THEY ALWAYS MANAGED TO PACK THE HOUSE, PROMPTING THE OWNER TO MUSE, "I WISH I COULD BOTTLE WHATEVER PANTERA HAS AND GIVE IT TO THE OTHER BANDS."

In Jerry's Words
"He'd Just Get Right Up There"

Wearing aviator sunglasses and a faraway grin, Jerry Abbott flips through the snapshots that document his son's career. One particular photo jars a memory, and as he taps at it with a meaty finger, the grin widens across his face.

"Darrell was really good about **SITTING IN** with people. He'd just get right up there, even way back when he was a **KID**. We used to go see this guy—Ricky Lynn Gregg—who was a killer singer, and he played a plenty fine rock 'n' roll guitar—plenty fine. And Darrell would **GET UP THERE** with his guitar and stand right beside him. Ricky Lynn would play some lick, and I would think, "Well, what's Darrell gonna do to follow that?" And he'd just play the same lick, and then maybe embellish around it for a minute, and then give it back to Ricky Lynn. And I'd think, "**I CAN'T BELIEVE** that little shit is standing up there doing that." If anybody wanted him to **JOIN IN** and be a part of something, he would do it. He **PARTICIPATED**. That's a part of his nature that some people don't know."

In 1986, the band performed at the Arcadia Theater in a sold-out blowout sponsored by the local radio station KZRK— known locally as Z-Rock. Fans lined the streets well in advance of the show to see the boys rock Dallas's vintage theater.

This early set list offers a taste of the cover tunes the boys played during their club days—plenty of hard rock and metal, but also a number of danceable tunes that were popular at the time. As the handwritten additions show, they were always learning new material to hone their skills and vary their performances.

Dime and Terry Glaze take center stage at a beach party. This was the first outdoor performance by the band, held at a recreation area called Sandy Beach on Lake Worth, a few miles outside of Fort Worth, Texas.

RIFFS OF STEEL:
DIME LETS LOOSE ON
THE WHAMMY BAR WITH A
SOUND SO RAW AND TACTILE
THAT THE FANS JUST WANT
TO GRAB ONTO IT.

SEVENTEEN-YEAR-OLD DARRELL ABBOTT PUTS HIS CHERISHED DEAN ML THROUGH ITS PACES FOR A HOMETOWN ARLINGTON AUDIENCE AT THE WORLD-FAMOUS SIX FLAGS OVER TEXAS AMUSEMENT PARK IN 1983. BY THIS TIME, THE AMAZING BOND BETWEEN DARRELL AND THE CROWDS TRANSCENDED ANY NORMAL CONNECTION BETWEEN PERFORMER AND FAN AS EVIDENCED IN THIS SERIES OF CANDID PHOTOS: THE FANS SEEM TO PULL DIME CLOSER THROUGH SHEER FORCE OF WILL; BUT, WHEN HE LEANS BACK, THEY SURGE FORWARD TO *MAINTAIN THE CONNECTION*. LIKE AGELESS PARTNERS IN AN ETERNAL DANCE, CROWD AND PERFORMER ARE IN PERFECT SYNC.

The band also did a show at Six Flags Over Texas in 1984. Over their objections, the park management relegated them to a secondary stage that had an attendance record of 1,700. When the band walked on stage to perform, an audience of 3,500 Texas head-bangers greeted them with a deafening chorus of shouts and cheers.

P.S.T. 88

Of course, **DIME** is best known for his groundbreaking guitar innovations, but in the band's early days, he also did some **SINGING**. While **STARTING OUT** on the club circuit, the band relied heavily on **COVERS**, and Dime regularly handled the vocals when they played Metallica songs. His rendition of "Seek and Destroy," which he sang as "Drink and Destroy," was a **FAVORITE** among fans.

He took over the vocal slot for **ONE AND ONLY ONE** recorded Pantera song—"P.S.T. 88." The final track on *Power Metal*, which is the first album the band did with Phil Anselmo, the **THRASH METAL** tune is notable for its frenetic drumming, strong riffs, and a blistering two-minute guitar solo. The **CRYPTIC LYRICS** are oddly self-reflexive and strive for a touch of wry **HUMOR**. As the band moved forward, Dime **GAVE UP SINGING** and focused all of his energy on **SHREDDING**. Years later, however, he wrote and sang "Rage in a Cage" for the action flick *Supercop*.

DARRELL WARMS UP BEFORE A SHOW AT WOODSTOCK, A CLUB IN KILLEEN, TEXAS, JUST DOWN THE ROAD FROM THE FORT HOOD ARMY BASE. THE CLUB WAS A HUGE METAL STRUCTURE WITH A CORRUGATED TIN ROOF AND A CONCRETE FLOOR WHERE SOLDIERS CAME TO BLOW OFF STEAM BY HEADBANGING TO SOME HOMEGROWN HEAVY METAL. DIME AND THE BAND WERE OFTEN BOOKED THERE FOR A WEEK (TUESDAY THROUGH SUNDAY), WHICH WAS A WELCOME BREAK FROM THE ONE-NIGHT STANDS.

DIME PLAYS HIS SOLO FROM "FLOODS" IN A PERFORMANCE AT SAVVY'S. HE HAD AN ARSENAL OF SOLOS, INCLUDING A TRIBUTE TO THE LATE RANDY RHOADS. HE'D PLAY SEGMENTS OF "DIARY OF A MADMAN" AND "YOU CAN'T KILL ROCK AND ROLL," THEN BURST INTO "SUICIDE SOLUTION."

DIME'S EXTENDED SOLOS WERE PARTICULARLY IMPRESSIVE TO SEE AT WOODSTOCK, AS THE LONE GUITARIST SATURATED THE ENORMOUS HALL WITH SOUND AND BROUGHT THE ROWDY CROWDS TO A FEVER PITCH. IT WASN'T UNCOMMON FOR HIM TO PLAY 15 OR 20 MINUTES WHILE THE REST OF THE BAND RESTED UP. OFTEN, HE WOULD BREAK INTO EDDIE VAN HALEN'S SIGNATURE GUITAR SOLO "ERUPTION," WITH THE ROLAND 201 ECHO DEVICE CRANKED ALL THE WAY UP.

What's in a Name

Over the years, several different stories about the origins of the band name Pantera have circulated. Here's the real deal, and remember—you read it here.

REJECTED NAMES Eternity; Gemini

WHO SUGGESTED PANTERA Donnie Sauers, a classmate of Vinnie's who knew him from the high school marching band

WHAT IT MEANS Yes, it means panther in Spanish, and the band's early logo included a big cat. But Donnie was something of a gear head and drew his inspiration from the badass Italian sports car designed by Alejandro De Tomaso. Vinnie and Dime didn't know about the Spanish meaning of the word until after they decided to go with the name.

WHY THEY PICKED IT It was easy to remember and, most importantly, it just sounded cool.

LOCATED IN A STRIP MALL ON EAST LANCASTER BLVD. IN FORT WORTH, SAVVY'S WAS NOT THE MOST GLAMOROUS CLUB IN TEXAS, BUT IT WAS AN IMPORTANT VENUE BECAUSE IT WAS A STEPPING STONE FOR MANY OF THE HARDROCK BANDS OF THE ERA. DARRELL WAS AT HOME THERE ON-STAGE AND BACKSTAGE (BOTTOM).

In 1983, Dime and Vinnie went to see Metallica at Harvey Hall in Tyler, Texas. It was Metallica's first tour through Texas, and there were no more than 50 people in attendance that night. The boys met James Hetfield and hung out. The next year, when Metallica was wrapping up the final leg of the Alcoholica Ride the Lightning tour, Hetfield was looking for some rest and relaxation and came down to Texas to hang out with Dime and Vinnie. The boys hit Savvy's where a jam session broke out, which then continued in the Abbotts' garage.

James plays Dime's Dean ML.

Two soon-to-be guitar legends tear it up.

New found friends.

Dime Destination
Pantego Sound

2310
Raper Boulevard
Pantego Texas

When **CHARLES STEWART** decided he wanted to take piano lessons, a friend suggested that a bandmate named **JERRY ABBOTT** might make a good teacher. After just a few lessons Jerry and Charles became **FAST FRIENDS**, brought together by their mutual passion for music.

Charles was a budding **MUSIC PRODUCER** who put out several singles with an up-and-coming local soul trio called The Van Dykes. Inspired by this early success, he decided to start up his own **RECORDING STUDIO** in Pantego, just outside of Fort Worth. Originally called Blue Royal Sound, the shop would later become known as **PANTEGO SOUND**. Charles took on a lanky young kid with an uncanny ear for music named T-Bone Burnett as his engineer. After just a few months, Burnett headed out for L.A., where he went on to become one of the most respected producers in the industry. Charles then **HIRED JERRY** to take over the **ENGINEERING** duties, and over the next several years Pantego grew into a respectable local recording and songwriting business.

During the 1970s, Jerry **BROUGHT VINNIE** and **DARRELL** to the studio regularly and **INTRODUCED** them to some of the most successful local performers in the area, including Texas blues legend Bugs Henderson and drummer Dahrell Norris. When the boys began working at their music seriously in the 1980s, Jerry's connection to Pantego Sound allowed the teens to work with **PROFESSIONAL** recording equipment right from the start. The band's **FIRST FIVE ALBUMS,** including *Cowboys from Hell*, were laid down and mixed with the MCI 500 console in the tiny studio on **RAPER BOULEVARD**.

VINNIE WORKS THE CONSOLE AT PANTEGO SOUND, WHILE MARC FERRARI OF KEEL HOLDS ONE OF DARRELL'S DEAN GUITARS. FERRARI WAS A CLOSE FRIEND TO THE ABBOTTS.

Jerry sits at the mixing board in Pantego Sound, where he produced the band's earliest recorded works. Jerry always referred to the band members as "the young'ns," and Dime, who was famous for slapping nicknames on people, started calling him "the Eld'n." Later, that tag would be shortened to "L.D."

OLD SCHOOL METAL RULES

Marc Ferrari was visiting Pantego while the boys recorded his metal anthem "Proud to be Loud" for their fourth album, Power Metal. Ferrari was impressed with Pantera and did his best to get a major label interested in them.

49

After Pantera started recording, they needed to find a way to get their disks distributed. Jerry and Vinnie went to Hastings Records and Tapes on the corner of Cooper Street and Park Row in Arlington and scribbled down a list of independent distributors taken from the backs of the heavy metal albums in the racks. A few letters and phone calls later, the band's recordings were being sold in foreign markets through a half dozen different channels.

Hastings is also where the band did their very first record signing, for the release of *Metal Magic*. The photos below capture the charisma, enthusiasm, and innocence of four young men who are just beginning to realize what their lives might become.

"THIS BAND COULD AND WOULD TAKE OVER THE THRONE OF COMMERCIAL METAL KINGS GIVEN THE RIGHT COMMERCIAL BACKIN'."

—DAVE CONSTABLE IN METAL FORCES MAGAZINE, VOLUME 14

It's a long way to the TOP!

Believe!

If you wanna Rock-N-Roll

BETWEEN 1983 AND 1988, THE BAND RELEASED FOUR INDEPENDENT ALBUMS THAT SOLD TENS OF THOUSANDS OF COPIES EACH.

PANTERA'S RECORDED WORK GENERALLY RECEIVED STELLAR REVIEWS IN THE OVERSEAS PRESS. THE BAND MADE THE COVER OF BRITAIN'S METAL FORCES, VOLUME 14, WHICH INCLUDED THIS REVIEW THAT SINGLES OUT DIME'S GUITAR WORK ON "COME ON EYES." STILL, A MAJOR-LABEL DEAL ELUDED THEM.

AT THE BRONCO BOWL IN 1985, DIME STEPS UP FOR HIS SOLO ON THE EARLY PANTERA TUNE "ALL OVER TONIGHT." THE BAND CHOSE THIS SONG FOR THEIR FIRST MUSIC VIDEO.

Getting It on Tape

The band selected the song "All Over Tonight" for their **FIRST VIDEO** because it had an overall heavy sound and because it gave **EACH MEMBER** a moment or two in the **SPOTLIGHT**. Darrell's **SOLO** was wicked, Vinnie did a brief but powerful roll on the **DRUMS**, Terry got to **STRETCH HIS RANGE** on the chorus, and the song had a nice open area where Rex's **BASS STOOD OUT**. It was perfect choice for showcasing the **MUSICIANSHIP** and **CHARISMA** of the young band.

They shot everything on a winter Sunday at the Rock of Texas, after having done a show there the night before. Their lights, smoke machine, and pyrotechnics were all still in place, and they **POURED** it all on during taping. Shooting took **ALL DAY** and into the **NIGHT**, and there was a hundred-mile drive home in a ten-year-old car with no heater waiting for them when they were done.

After several weeks of **EDITING**, they sent the video to **MTV** with **HOPES** of finally getting some attention outside Texas, but it **NEVER HAPPENED**—you didn't get airtime from cable's music giant without major-label backing.

VOCAL ROULETTE

In the mid 1980s, singer Terry Glaze decided to leave Pantera for a band called Lord Tracy, who had just signed a record deal with MCA. Before hooking up with Phil Anselmo, Dime, Vinnie, and Rex went through a string of frontmen who just didn't work out.

1 **DONNIE HART** was a school friend of Vinnie's with a hard-rock voice who couldn't manage to put the necessary time into working with the band.

2 **DAVID PEACOCK** had a distinctive vocal style but found his voice couldn't quite hold up to performances night after night.

3 **MATT LAMOUR** came from Houston with a great reputation but he didn't click with the band; today he fronts a popular Led Zeppelin tribute band.

4 Stuck in El Paso one night without a singer, Pantera let an energetic audience member with decent pipes (whose name remains unknown) perform with them, and he totally tore up the stage. When the band agreed to let him continue gigging with them, the **WANNABE ROCKER** spent the next 24 hours partying to celebrate his arrival at the top of the local music scene. The next night, a few songs into the first set, he collapsed from heart failure on stage and had to be wheeled out by paramedics.

ONSTAGE AND OFF, DIME WAS THE SOURCE OF ENERGY THAT FUELED THE BAND. HERE, TERRY AND DIME RIP IT UP AT SAVVY'S ON THE *I AM THE NIGHT* TOUR, 1985-1986. TERRY SPORTS THE OFFICIAL TOUR T-SHIRT.

THE LOCAL CLUB CIRCUIT WAS IN MANY WAYS JUST AS GRUELING AS A NATIONAL TOUR—CRAMMING ALL THEIR GEAR INTO A CAR, DRIVING FOR HOURS, SETTING UP BEFORE THE SHOW, AND PUTTING ON A HIGH-ENERGY PERFORMANCE, ONLY TO HAVE TO BREAK THE SET DOWN AND MAKE THE DRIVE BACK HOME AGAIN. DIME LEARNED EARLY THAT HUMOR WAS THE BEST WAY TO LIGHTEN THE PRESSURE AND FRUSTRATION, AND HE ALWAYS FOUND A WAY TO MAKE SURE EVERYBODY HAD A GOOD TIME WHILE THEY WERE WORKING.

COWBOYS FROM HELL
Rock Stars

During the late 1980s, Jerry and the band continued to work hard to secure a record contract with a major label, but that goal remained elusive. One day, a representative from Mechanix Records called and offered to sign Pantera to a record deal. Jerry turned him down but came away from the conversation with some excellent advice. The record exec complimented the band's diversity but remarked that it could be working against

CHAPTER 4

BEING ON TOUR AND RECORDING IN THE STUDIO DEFINED
THE LIFE OF DARRELL AND THE BAND AFTER THEY SIGNED
WITH ATCO.

them. He recommended the band pick one musical direction and pour all of their creativity into pursuing it. The advice was exactly what the boys wanted to hear. Their last album, *Power Metal*, had benefited from a harder, faster sound, and the band was excited by the response. They charged forward toward the heaviest of metal music—and they never looked back.

THE BAND GREW INCREASINGLY FRUSTRATED WHEN THEY HAD NOT SECURED A MAJOR RECORDING DEAL BY THE END OF THE 1980s.

Derek Shulman of Polygram Records (a division of Atlantic, or Atco) had been keeping tabs on Pantera since their first album on the Metal Magic label, thinking some day he might sign them. After Shulman heard the blistering sounds of *Power Metal*, plus an advance tape of the band's latest work, the wheels were finally set in motion—with a little help from Hurricane Hugo. Atco record exec Mark Ross was en route to the Southeast to see a band called Tangiers, but Hurricane Hugo sidetracked his plane to Dallas. He phoned Shulman to explain that he was grounded in Texas, and Shulman immediately suggested he go see Pantera while there.

By this point, the boys had grown weary of getting their hopes up with record executives only to have the deals fall through at the last minute. When Ross called Vinnie to let him know he was in town and asked what he could expect from his band, the cheeky drummer boasted that they could be the next Metallica and suggested that Ross check them out at a private birthday party they were playing in a Fort Worth disco.

Ross did show up, but after a couple of songs, he quietly slipped out the door. Vinnie and Darrell thought it was just another case of a record exec with no ears and kicked the festivities into high gear. Soon, the drinks were flowing, the guests were partying, and birthday cake was flying through the air. A half hour later, the band was shocked to see Ross stroll back in. He had been so blown away by the band's first few songs, he rushed out to call the label and tell them he was signing Pantera right there on the spot—which he did.

The band was signed to Atco's East-West subsidiary. After they laid down a few tracks for their next album, Shulman came down to see them play at Joe's Garage in Fort Worth to check out his investment and to witness the electricity of a live performance firsthand. If he did not yet know that Darrell would be the next big influence on metal guitar, then he at least sensed the band's potential for success. And he was right; Ross signed 18 other groups at about this same time but Pantera was the only band to succeed and the only band to reach the top.

The boys' 1990 debut album on a major label was not just a major metal hit, it was groundbreaking. *Cowboys from Hell* featured the fierce aggressive style that became their stock in trade, and it came

along at a time when other metal bands had begun softening their sound. The hard and fast thrash metal style they had started to hone with *Power Metal* matured on *Cowboys from Hell*. The addition of Phil Anselmo enabled the band to go as hard and heavy as they wanted to. His deep, powerful vocals complemented Darrell's tuned-down guitar to create a dark, menacing sound. In a 1990 interview in *Guitar World*, Darrell announced that they were playing a new groove now, and they labeled it the power groove.

Vinnie had begun developing his chops as an engineer on their recordings before *Cowboys from Hell*, helping Darrell to achieve the fierce guitar

TERRY DATE (FAR RIGHT) COPRODUCED PANTERA'S ALBUMS ON THE ATCO LABEL. HERE HE WORKS WITH THE BOYS ON *VULGAR DISPLAY OF POWER* AT PANTEGO SOUND STUDIO IN ARLINGTON. THE ALBUMS WERE BUILT AROUND THE MUSICAL ATHLETICISM OF DARRELL'S BRILLIANT FRETWORK AND VINNIE'S SPEED-OF-LIGHT PRECISION DRUMMING, WHICH WAS COMPLEMENTED BY REX BROWN'S BASSWORK. THOUGH COMPLETELY NONMELODIC, PHIL'S VOICE FROM THE ABYSS ADDED A COURSE TEXTURE TO THEIR SOUND THAT MADE IT RAW AND REAL.

sound he wanted. After signing with Atco, the band got additional engineering support through Terry Date, an experienced producer of hard-rocking-bands such as Soundgarden, White Zombie, and Prong. Date flew down to Texas to help them record at Pantego Sound, bringing with him additional equipment that was made to order for a heavy metal band. Date helped the band hone their sound and sharpen their talents. Darrell's riffs on "The Art of Shredding" propelled him to the big leagues alongside the likes of Metallica's James Hetfield and Megadeth's Dave Mustaine, while his amazing work on "Cemetery Gates" revealed a soulful side to metal.

With Darrell shredding in the power groove, Vinnie pounding the skins with greater precision than ever, Rex pulverizing the low end, and Phil growling the vocals, *Cowboys from Hell* was miles away from glam metal. Phil and Darrell felt it was time to ditch the poodle perms, torn t-shirts, spandex pants, and yards of scarves. Vinnie was reluctant to give up the look but eventually relented when Dime reminded him that the magic clothes didn't make the music, they did. The band's dedicated

fan base agreed and eagerly embraced the power groove when the group hit the road on their first major tour. One leg of the tour went international when the boys were asked to join one of the icons of metal—Judas Priest—on tour in Europe.

If *Cowboys from Hell* introduced a more aggressive Pantera, then *Vulgar Display of Power* painted them as the vanguard of extreme metal. With such tracks as "Mouth for War" and "Fucking Hostile," the album's sound was muscular, masculine, and just on the verge of meltdown. By this time, everyone—fans, friends, the press, record execs—knew Darrell as Dimebag, and they expected him to break out with bone-shattering guitar riffs, innovative solos, and his distinct razor-sharp tone. His fast and furious guitar work was indelibly linked to his brother's equally fast and crushing drumming style—a style that earned Vinnie the nickname "Vinnie Paul, the Brick Wall." Incredibly in sync both onstage and off, the Abbott Brothers brought an unmistakable synergy that added power and depth to Pantera's influential sound.

The band maintained an incredible pace through the 1990s, touring nonstop and releasing album after

DIME COMMEMORATED THE *COWBOYS FROM HELL* ALBUM WITH AN ORIGINAL TATTOO.

album of the most aggressive metal in history even as the mainstream music industry began turning its back on metal. Seeking to out-power *Vulgar Display*, the group rocked harder and faster on their next album, *Far Beyond Driven*, in 1994. To the music industry's surprise and dismay, *Far Beyond Driven* debuted at *number one* on The Billboard 200, becoming the first heavy metal album in history to do so. Their fan base—among the most loyal in metal history—had come through to defy the expectations of the music industry, which did not fully understand or respect heavy metal. *Driven* was followed by *The Great Southern Trendkill*, which served as a message to fans and others that Pantera was out to buck the trend of many of their contemporaries who were drifting away from the "heavy" in heavy metal. To support the albums, feature-length videos—including footage shot by Dime—were released to give the fans something extra, because MTV and other music-video outlets were not offering any airplay or attention. The band rounded out the decade with a powerful live album, *Official Live: 101 Proof*, which also included two new studio cuts, "Where You Come From" and "I Can't Hide."

The boys ushered in the new millennium with *Reinventing the Steel*. The title offered an homage to Judas Priest's old-school metal sound from their album *British Steel*. Though the cuts included fewer solos from Dime, he attracted attention from the rock press for his use of sound processing on the opening riff in "Hellbound." "Revolution Is My Name" earned the group their fourth Grammy nomination for Best Metal Performance, while "We'll Grind That

Axe for a Long Time" expressed their dedication to the spirit and style of pure heavy metal.

Reinventing the Steel turned out to be the band's last album, except for two greatest hits compilations, *The Best of Pantera: Far Beyond The Great Southern Cowboys' Vulgar Hits* and *Reinventing Hell: The Best of Pantera*. Through an unfortunate series of events stretched out over a few years, the band dissolved circa 2002–2003 after tension between Phil Anselmo

WHEN YOU BUY A PANTERA ALBUM, YOU'RE GOING TO GET BLUDGEONED....

—ZAKK WYLDE,
VH1 BEHIND THE MUSIC: PANTERA

and the rest of the band members evolved into irreconcilable differences. In addition to Anselmo's increasingly erratic, unprofessional behavior—including a heroin overdose in 1996—outside

interests had pulled him away from the band. Along with some veterans of other metal bands, Anselmo had formed a group called Down in the mid-1990s to pursue that dark subgenre dubbed doom metal. His growling voice and penchant for gloomy, self-absorbed lyrics were suited to that fringe end of the metal spectrum. In addition, he was part of an under-ground metal band called Superjoint Ritual, which surfaced "above ground" in 2000 with an album that let the gravel-throated singer indulge his punk-rock influences. It became increasingly difficult to get Anselmo to focus on Pantera; he had disconnected from the band, and bassist Rex Brown went with him. After a 2001 Pantera tour was cut short by the events of 9/11, the Abbott Brothers were anxious to return to recording or touring, but Anselmo was unrespon-sive. Eventually, it became clear he had no intention of returning, though no formal announcement of his decision was forthcoming. Legally, the name Pantera could not be used by any members of the band without the consent of all the members of the band. As a result, the band that Vinnie Paul and Darrell had cofounded and poured their lives into ceased to ex-ist, a fact that pained Darrell until his untimely death.

NEW NEIL YOUNG | JOE SATRIANI | LOU REED | KISS

GUITAR WORLD

DIMEBAG DARRELL says:

OLD SCHOOL METAL RULES

LET THERE BE ROCK!
AC/DC
HIGH-VOLTAGE LESSON WITH ANGUS YOUNG
PLUS: AC/DC'S 10 GREATEST RIFFS

KITTIE
FASTER PUSSYCAT
KILL! KILL!

STEVIE RAY VAUGHAN
NEW ALBUM!
PLUS: EXCLUSIVE INTERVIEW WITH DOUBLE TROUBLE

IT'S PANTERA, BABY!
DIMEBAG DARRELL SAVES HEAVY METAL

MAY 2000

MANY, INCLUDING *GUITAR WORLD* MAGAZINE, ACKNOWLEDGE THE DEBT OWED TO DIME AND PANTERA FOR KEEPING METAL "HEAVY" DURING THE 1990S.

Heavy metal music had not heard the last of the Abbott Brothers. They would return in full force with their new band, Damageplan. Yet it is important to recognize and appreciate Pantera's place in metal history. The band's first album for a major label, *Cowboys from Hell*, came along at a time when metal music was in decline. After regularly hitting the charts for the preceding decade, metal began to lose its hold on the mainstream audiences in the early 1990s. The music industry and the entertainment press chased after the Seattle grunge scene at the expense of other, established genres of music, and some metal bands softened or altered their sound as a result. But Pantera stayed true to their passions, keeping the aggression and fierceness of heavy metal alive. As Scott Ian of Anthrax succinctly put it, "Pantera saved metal."

DARRELL'S FIERY FRETWORK
AND SMOLDERING SOLOS
DURING LIVE PERFORMANCES,
PLUS THE UNDERGROUND
SUCCESS OF *POWER METAL*,
HELPED THE BAND GET
SIGNED TO A NATIONALLY
BASED LABEL AND ATTRACT
THE ATTENTION OF A MAJOR
MANAGEMENT COMPANY.

Dime Destination Campo Verde

WALTER O'BRIEN and **ANDY GOULD** of Concrete Management (who Dime later dubbed "The Piranha Brothers") became **PANTERA'S MANAGEMENT COMPANY** not long after they signed with Atco. Together, with the assistance of Kim Zide, they guided the band through the 1990s, booking them all over the world. Concrete Management was a relatively new company, having formed in 1989, but it had a reputation for representing major heavy metal bands, including White Zombie. O'Brien **SIGNED THE MANAGEMENT AGREEMENT** with Darrell, Vinnie, Rex, and Phil at this corner table in a Mexican restaurant called **CAMPO VERDE**, which was one of **DIME'S FAVORITE** eateries.

Located on Pioneer Parkway in Arlington, Texas, Campo Verde's uniquely festive décor gives new meaning to the phrase **LOCAL COLOR**. Christmas lights adorn the interior all year around, and a model train circles the restaurant along a tiny track a few feet above diners' heads. Skulls, neon cacti, and Native American pottery add the obligatory western flavor. Darrell frequented the restaurant with friends, family, and other musicians, often treating them to **RATTLESNAKE** and **TEQUILA**— a true Texas delicacy.

GIVEN DARRELL'S RISK-TAKING RIFFS AS A GUITAR SLINGER, IT SHOULD COME AS NO SURPRISE THAT ANOTHER FAVORITE DIME DESTINATION WAS LAS VEGAS, GAMBLING MECCA OF AMERICA. FROM THE VERY BEGINNING OF HIS SUCCESS, HE WAS LURED TO VEGAS BY HIS LOVE OF BLACKJACK. HE WAS FAMOUS FOR GIVING A FELLOW GAMBLER WHO WENT BUST A NEW STAKE. HE WOULD SMILE, BUY THE DUDE A DRINK, LAY A FRESH STACK OF CHIPS IN FRONT OF HIM, AND ADVISE HIM TO "GETCHA PULL"—ONE OF DIME'S LEGENDARY EXPRESSIONS.

THE KEY TO THE LOYALTY OF
HEAVY METAL FANS IS FEELING
CONNECTED TO THE BAND, AND
THAT CONNECTION STARTS WITH
A RAGING SHOWMANSHIP THAT
MATCHES THE HEAD-BANGING
AGGRESSION OF THE AUDIENCE.
DIME'S SHOWMANSHIP TURNED
ANY CONCERT INTO THE THRASH
OF THE TITANS.

Ín Vinnie's Words
"Ain't Doing It Without My Brother"

It's an unusually warm autumn afternoon somewhere in Indiana, and Vinnie kills time in the back of the tour bus with the a/c cranked high, just the way he likes it. In a couple of hours, he'll be back in the spotlight hammering the skins for yet another cheering throng of fans. He thinks back to a day 18 years earlier when it all could have fallen apart, and he tells the story with a smile:

Vinnie recalls, **"DAVE MUSTAINE** called [Dime] up and and said, **'HEY, DUDE, OUR GUITAR PLAYER JUST QUIT**….You're the guy. Check it out, dude. You get a Nike endorsement. You'll have insurance. You're gonna get a paycheck….We'll be out playing with the likes of Metallica, Slayer, Iron Maiden, and all your fuckin' favorite bands. **ALL YOU GOTTA DO IS JUST SAY YES**….' [Dime] goes, 'Dave, every bit of that sounds good, exactly what I want to do, but there's one condition, man—**AIN'T DOING IT WITHOUT MY BROTHER**.' Dave said, 'We already have a drummer.' So Dime came to me, 'Dude, what should I do?' It was a hard decision for him, you know….And I said, 'You gotta do what you gotta do for a livin' and I ain't gonna blame you one way or another.' But **I WAS FREAKIN'**. The next day after the call came in from Dave, I was sitting there and I said, 'What happened?' And, he said, 'I just told Dave straight up, **EITHER YOU'RE COMING OR WE AIN'T COMING AT ALL**.'

DIME HAS THE "BLUES" AT MANGO'S
IN GRAND PRAIRIE, TEXAS, CIRCA MID-
1990'S. NICK BOWCOTT, AN ASSOCIATE
EDITOR FOR *GUITAR WORLD,* TOLD THE
BALTIMORE SUN THAT DARRELL AND
THE BAND WERE THE MOST IMPORTANT
METAL ACT OF THE 1990S.

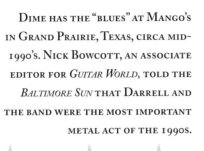

KERRY KING OF SLAYER JAMS WITH
DIME ONSTAGE AT JOE'S GARAGE IN
FT. WORTH, CIRCA 1989. THE PHOTO
CAPTURES THE HIGH POINT OF THE
GIG WHEN THEY WERE REALLY RIP-
PING THE JOINT APART.

"IT WAS A WHOLE NEW ANIMAL. UNBELIEVABLY POWERFUL. UNDENIABLY FIERCE AS HELL."

–JERRY CANTRELL OF ALICE IN CHAINS ON COWBOYS FROM HELL

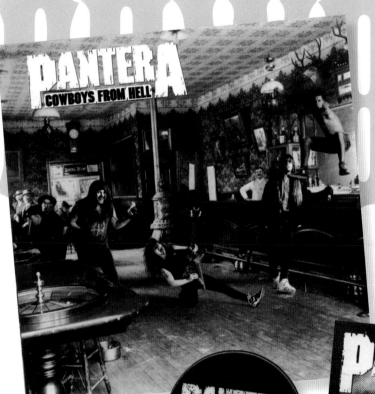

COWBOYS FROM HELL, RELEASED IN JULY 1990, FEATURED A HARD-CORE SOUND THAT BORE THE INFLUENCE OF THRASH METAL BANDS OF THE PREVIOUS DECADE, SUCH AS SLAYER AND METALLICA. YET IT POINTED THE WAY TO THE POWER METAL THAT WOULD BE PANTERA'S CONTRIBUTION TO METAL HISTORY. FROM THE INSTANTLY RECOGNIZABLE OPENING RIFF ON THE TITLE TRACK TO THE POWER SHREDDING ON "DOMINATION," DARRELL'S GUITAR WORK DEFINED THE BAND'S DIRECTION. "CEMETERY GATES," WHICH IS BUILT AROUND A BLISTERING GUITAR RIFF AND A HAUNTING, SOULFUL SOLO, BECAME PANTERA'S BEST-KNOWN BALLAD, PARTICULARLY IN RETROSPECT.

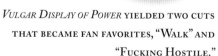

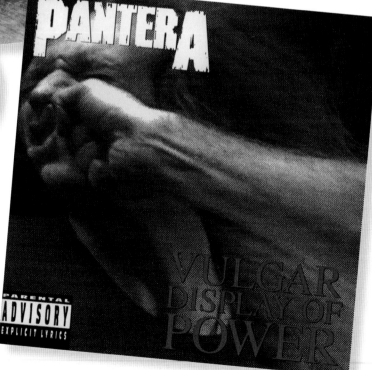

VULGAR DISPLAY OF POWER YIELDED TWO CUTS THAT BECAME FAN FAVORITES, "WALK" AND "FUCKING HOSTILE."

THE Billboard 200

FOR WEEK ENDING
APRIL 9, 1994

THIS WEEK	LAST WEEK	2 WKS AGO	WKS. ON CHART	ARTIST LABEL & NUMBER/DISTRIBUTING LABEL (SUGGESTED LIST PRICE OR EQUIVALENT FOR CASSETTE/CD)	TITLE	PEAK POSITION
				★★★ No. 1/Hot Shot Debut ★★★ FAR BEYOND DRIVEN		1
1	NEW ▶		1	PANTERA EASTWEST 92302*/AG (10.98/15.98) 1 week at No. 1	LONGING IN THEIR HEARTS	2
2	NEW ▶		1	BONNIE RAITT CAPITOL 81427 (10.98/16.98)	THE SIGN	1
				ACE OF BASE ▲² ARISTA 18740 (9.98/15.98)	ABOVE THE RIM	4
		3	18	SOUNDTRACK DEATH ROW/INTERSCOPE 92359/AG (10.98/16.98)	LIVE AT THE ACROPOLIS	5
				...92116 (10.98/15.98)	12 PLAY	2
					...ST & EVERYTHING AFTER	4
					SUPERUNKNOWN	1
					MUSIC BOX	1
					THE COLOUR OF MY LOVE	4
					TONI BRAXTON	1

THIS WEEK	LAST WEEK	2 WKS AGO	WKS. ON CHART	ARTIST LABEL & NUMBER/DISTRIBUTING LABEL
56	44	43	7	ZHANE ILLTOWN 6369/MOTOWN (
57	52	55	30	GARTH BROOKS ▲⁴ LIBERTY
58	41	41	26	REBA MCENTIRE ▲² MCA 10
59	48	47	7	RICHARD MARX CAPITOL 8123
60	49	48	22	10,000 MANIACS ▲ ELEKTRA
(61)	66	65	16	DOMINO ● OUTBURST/CHAOS 5
62	50	46	44	ROD STEWART ▲² WARNER
63	61	60	17	CRACKER ● VIRGIN 39012 (9.9
64	58	51	50	GIN BLOSSOMS ▲ A&M 5403
				SARAH MCLACHLAN ARISTA
(65)	78	95	6	LITTLE TEXAS ● WARNER BR
66	59	62	45	PEARL JAM ▲⁶ EPIC 47857 (1(
67	63	64	119	

The skull with a drill bit driven into it, which graces the cover of *Far Beyond Driven*, perfectly symbolizes the head-crushing sounds of Pantera's third album for Atco. Dime's guitar licks scream and Vinnie's drumming pulverizes, while Phil roars some of the bleakest lyrics ever to grace an album. While many metal bands worked hard to embrace a style—thrash, speed, or death metal—Pantera defied simple categorization by pushing its sound to the end of the line without losing control, which is the hallmark of artistry. Small wonder this disk sold 185,907 copies in its first week to debut in the *number-one* spot on the Billboard 200 chart—a first for any heavy metal album.

DIMEBAG

In the April 1992 issue of *Guitar World*, the youngest Abbott brother officially announced his preference for a different nickname, Dimebag Darrell. Dime was never crazy about the nickname Diamond Darrell, primarily because there was Diamond David Lee Roth of Van Halen. He needed something more distinct. In the parlance of the counter-culture, a dimebag is a ten-dollar bag of marijuana. In the parlance of rock 'n' roll, he knew he had found exactly what he was looking for when he stumbled across the idea of "Dimebag" Darrell—it was one word that would connect with the bohemian masses who love metal. Almost instantly, the name became mythic among fans—a single word that summed up the **musical genius and raucous spirit of a living metal legend.**

Dime takes a break from recording *Vulgar Display of Power* at Pantego Sound Studio to get a little crazy. He liked to create a party atmosphere wherever he was, which relaxed everyone else and turned any activity into fun. Like a typical little brother, Darrell could also coerce Vinnie into the act. *Vulgar* was the last Pantera album to be recorded at Pantego Sound Studio. For the album *Far Beyond Driven*, the band chose to lay down the tracks at Abtrax Recording in Nashville (LD's new studio); Phil's vocals were done at Trent Reznor's in New Orleans, and the album was mixed at Dallas Sound Lab. Afterward, all material was recorded in the studio Dime had constructed behind his new house in Arlington.

MORE FAMOUS FRIENDS

ROCKERS SAMMY HAGAR AND
MICHAEL ANTHONY (FORMERLY
OF VAN HALEN) GREET THE
ABBOTT BROTHERS.

RICK NIELSEN OF CHEAP
TRICK BROUGHT HIS SON
TO SEE PANTERA IN HIS
HOMETOWN OF PEORIA,
ILLINOIS. BOTH FATHER
AND SON WERE BIG FANS.

DIME AND DUG PINNICK OF KING'S X
RESPECTED AND ADMIRED EACH OTHER'S
WORK.

BILLY CORGAN AND JAMES IHA FROM THE SMASHING PUMPKINS WENT BACKSTAGE AT CHICAGO'S ROSEMONT HORIZON TO MEET VINNIE AND DIME, CIRCA 2000.

KID ROCK INVITED DIME, VINNIE, AND KID'S WHOLE CREW TO DINNER AFTER A SHOW. KID PAID THE $2000 TAB AND DIME LEFT A $700 TIP.

DIME HAD HEARD ABOUT JOEY BUTTAFUOCO FROM THE WALL-TO-WALL MEDIA COVERAGE SURROUNDING THE SHOOTING OF HIS WIFE BY HIS TEENAGE GIRLFRIEND. WHILE IN NEW YORK, DIME ASKED HIS LIMO DRIVER TO TAKE HIM TO BUTTAFUOCO'S AUTO BODY BUSINESS IN BALDWIN, NEW YORK. THE ROCK GUITARIST STROLLED INTO BUTTAFUOCO'S SHOP, INTRODUCED HIMSELF, AND INVITED THE NOTORIOUS CELEBRITY TO A PARTY. DIME NEVER MET A BUTTAFUOCO HE DIDN'T LIKE.

Loaded with attitude, *The Great Southern Trendkill* was the band's answer to the music industry's tendency to fall for trends, fads, and crazes. Dime summed it up in the September 1996 issue of *Guitar Player*, "If you look at what's going on today, you've got all these dudes with two or three strings on their guitars, playing one- or two-chord songs, whatever the month might be. Come on, man—that ain't fuckin' jammin.'"

Official Live: 101 Proof was the band's no-holds-barred concert album, which also featured two studio cuts, "Where You Come From" and "I Can't Hide."

Reinventing the Steel, released in 2000, showcased the musical athleticism of Dime's guitar work and Vinnie's relentlessly intense drumming. An homage to Judas Priest's *British Steel*, the album was the last for Pantera, save for the greatest hits album, *The Best of Pantera: Far Beyond the Great Southern Cowboys Vulgar Hits*.

The Grammys and Pantera

1994 NOMINATION FOR BEST METAL PERFORMANCE FOR I'M BROKEN

1996 NOMINATION FOR BEST METAL PERFORMANCE FOR SUICIDE NOTE PT. I

1997 NOMINATION FOR BEST METAL PERFORMANCE FOR CEMETERY GATES

2000 NOMINATION FOR BEST METAL PERFORMANCE FOR REVOLUTION IS MY NAME

"WE LOOK AT OUR MUSIC AS **BALL-BUSTING,** GUT-WRENCHING HEAVY.... WE'RE A SUPER-**AGGRESSIVE** BAND AND ALL OUR SONGS ARE MEANT TO BE PLAYED **LIVE.** WE PLAY A **NEW** GROOVE—WE CALL IT 'POWER GROOVE.' WE'RE LIKE FINE-TUNED, **CLEAN-CUTTING MACHINERY.**"

—DIMEBAG DARRELL,
QUOTED IN GUITAR WORLD, MARCH 2005

THE ROAD
Onward We Rock

Fans of heavy metal know that you don't just listen to the music—
you experience it. From the chest-pounding roar of the drums to the ear-
shattering wail of the soaring guitar solo, metal demands to be experienced live. The power and energy of the band onstage is absorbed by the
crowd, who return it through head-banging, stage diving, and moshing.
The interaction between band and audience forms a tight bond that makes

RIGHT, DIME BASKS IN THE ADULATION OF THE CROWDS WHO FLOCKED FROM NEAR AND FAR
TO HEAR HIM ROCK THE HOUSE, WHILE THE ABOVE PHOTO REVEALS THE TYPE OF STRANGE
PLACES A ROCK 'N' ROLLER CAN END UP AT WHILE ON TOUR.

CHAPTER 5

metal fans the most devoted in popular music and metal musicians among the most appreciative. Thus, touring is the backbone of heavy metal, creating a sense of community among fans that is unique in popular music. In other words, it all boils down to THE ROAD.

A HEAVY METAL CONCERT IS LIKE AN ANCIENT ARENA, WHERE RAW ENERGY AND BRUTE FORCE ARE GENERATED, EXPERIENCED, AND THEN SHARED BY THE AUDIENCE AND THE BAND. AND IN THE ARENA OF METAL, DIME WAS A WARRIOR.

Pantera built its reputation and career on live performances, earning the devotion of fans who remained loyal through the decades, passing on their passion to new generations. Ask anyone about Pantera's fans, and the word that inevitably comes up is "die-hard." With little help from radio and none

from MTV, the band earned its success the old-fashioned way—continuous touring fueled by word of mouth among those diehard fans.

> "...WE DO IT THE OLD-SCHOOL WAY, THE WAY THEY USED TO DO IT. AND THAT'S JUST WORD-OF-MOUTH ... THAT'S THE WAY TO BE AROUND FOR TEN YEARS."
>
> —VINNIE, SEATTLE POST INTELLIGENCER, FEB. 9, 2001

Though the band had been a Texas favorite for years, touring for the *Cowboys from Hell* album launched them into international arenas, with a little help from friends in high places. While Pantera was headlining in Canada in 1990, Rob Halford of Judas

PÄINKILLER
TOUR 91
Judas Priest
PANTERA
ANNIHILATOR

ZAGREB,
26. 2. 1991,
DOM
SPORTOVA,
20.00

PRODAJA ULAZNICA PODHODNIK
• KOMPAS, OKC, INTEGRAL

300 DIN   № 000474

Priest saw them in a club called Rock & Roll Heaven in Toronto. Halford became so enthusiastic during the show that he climbed onstage to perform a couple of Priest tunes with the band and then invited Pantera to join Judas Priest on the European leg of the Painkiller Tour.

Excited to be playing with a band they considered an inspiration, the Cowboys from Hell embarked on a three-month tour of Europe—home to some of the world's biggest metalheads. Unfortunately, by the time the tour ended, the entire band felt more like the Cowboys in Hell. Money was tight on that first international tour so the boys shared a double-decker bus with a Canadian band called Annihilator. In total, 18 young men traveled together on one bus, often for weeks at a time. During one 60-day stretch, the boys were able to stay in a hotel only one time. Tempers flared and tension frequently erupted between the members of the two bands. In addition, the European audiences were cool toward Pantera, partly because they were new and partly because there was lingering anti-American sentiment left over from the first Gulf War. On that dismal tour, the most merchandise that was sold

at any one concert was in San Sebastian, Spain, where a grand total of 12 fans bought t-shirts.

Western Europe may have failed to appreciate Pantera, but the following year, the Russian fans—in the process of being liberated from Soviet Communism—made up for it. As part of the historic Monsters of Rock show, the band opened for Metallica and AC/DC at the Tushino Airfield near Moscow.

Eventually, the rest of Europe came to see that Dime and the band were the real deal. After the success of *Vulgar Display of Power*, European venues were begging the band to tour, but the boys were understandably reluctant to return to the Old Country. Finally, they agreed to tour with a band that Dime not only admired but had once considered joining, Megadeth. This time the response from the European crowds was enormous as Pantera assaulted their senses with thunderous fury.

Bigger successes prompted longer tours. The Far Beyond Driven tour of 1994–1995 consisted of 297 dates, with the band traveling everywhere but India,

China, and the Middle East. Pantera headlined each stage of the tour, and the venues were almost always sold out. The widely touted Extreme Steel Tour of 2001 would be the band's last, though no one knew it at the time, and it featured Pantera, Slayer, Static-X, Skrape, Nothingface, and Morbid Angel, among others. As the line-up suggests, the idea behind the tour was to bring together bands with the most brutal, hard-core metal sounds. Touring with Slayer seemed a natural, because not only did axe-man Kerry King make a guest appearance on *Reinventing the Steel*, but the band had innovated a raw, abrasive metal sound that fused a punk-rock attitude and brevity with metal's brutality and volume, which complemented Pantera's musical ferocity. Vinnie dubbed the tour "Panterafest."

Hitting the road with the likes of Judas Priest, Megadeth, and Slayer reveals one of the most stimulating aspects of touring—sharing the stage with the biggest stars of metal. Dime and Vinnie never tired of meeting and playing with those metal gods who had inspired them to pursue their passion. In 1997, they not only toured with KISS—Darrell's first metal heroes—but they were asked to open for the reunion tour of the original members of Black Sabbath.

Playing with the giants of metal, communing with fans, and drinking hard with old bandmates and newfound friends may make the road sound like an endless party. Yet touring can also be brutal because of endless nights on a bus, unfamiliar customs in strange lands, and long stretches of time away from the home. Darrell excelled at keeping up everyone's spirits and squeezing as much fun out of life on the road as humanly possible.

THE PARTY WAS ALWAYS ON DIME'S SHOULDERS, ESPECIALLY WHEN ON THE ROAD.

DIME, WHO WAS A BORN SHOWDOG, WAS NOT ABOVE USING A PROP ONSTAGE TO ENTERTAIN THE AUDIENCE.

As "Dimebag," Darrell became legendary for hosting the party backstage, onstage, and even on the bus, pouring his signature Black-Tooth Grins for everyone. He always loved the genial atmosphere and community spirit of a party, and eventually it became expected that he would keep the good times rolling every night. With the Crown Royal and Seagram's 7 flowing, Dime often took the party to the edge of chaos, engaging in such antics as paying partiers to down entire bottles of hot sauce. One Chicago-based disc jockey recalled Dime spray-painting the deejay's hair bright pink during the after-show party, while a rock reporter recalled the band giving free haircuts aboard the bus after a gig in Rockford, Illinois.

The most difficult part of life on the road is the down time during a long tour, and staying entertained is the only way to combat the monotony. Visiting the local malls often provided a distraction for Darrell, who loved to shop. And he spent many hours recording the band's adventures on video. Dime could also serve as a sort of master of ceremonies of the road, constantly entertaining others by pulling pranks, dreaming up crazy stunts, and manu-facturing his unique style of fun. During one tour, Dime had the crew rig a vampire doll to the back of the arena; then at a key moment, the doll came flying onstage, much to the surprise of the rest of the band. Thereafter, the doll was sometimes lit on fire before making its entrance on stage as one long streak of flames Once, someone rigged a walkie-talkie radio inside the doll, which was then stationed on a chair outside the bus. When an unsuspecting person walked by, Dime shouted into his radio, creating the illusion that the doll was speaking up. Inevitably, the passers-by freaked out, and Dime and his cohorts cracked up.

Some musicians can handle the road, some can't. But to Darrell and Vinnie, the road was a special place where the fans, the music, and their favorite bands all came together to celebrate the music industry's wildest outlaw son—heavy metal.

ON THEIR FIRST BIG TOUR AFTER
SIGNING WITH A MAJOR LABEL,
DARRELL TAKES THE SPOTLIGHT AT
THE ARCADIA THEATER IN DALLAS.
ON THIS LEG, PANTERA TOURED
WITH WRATHCHILD AMERICA,
AND DIME SHOWS HIS SUPPORT
BY SPORTING WRATHCHILD
MERCHANDISE.

OZZFEST!

Ozzfest represented a big break for Pantera. Sharon Osbourne founded this all-day heavy-metal festival in 1996 after the organizers of Lollapalooze refused to let Osbourne join the tour. The idea was to feature Ozzy as the main act with a variety of young metal bands filling out the bill. The 1996 Ozzfest did not tour but was instead a two-day event held in Phoenix, Arizona, and Devore, California. The following year, Osbourne organized a touring event, and most consider this the first true Ozzfest. Pantera was part of that historic, inaugural Ozzfest in 1997. They returned to tour with Ozzfest in 1998 and 2000. In 2003, Dime and Vinnie made a guest appearance at Ozzfest 2003 in Alpine Valley, Wisconsin, to join Disturbed for a version of "Walk."

AT THE 1998 OZZFEST, VINNIE AND DIME WATCH BLACK SABBATH FROM THE SIDE OF THE STAGE. PANTERA THEN BECAME THE OPENING ACT FOR BLACK SABBATH'S REUNION TOUR, WHICH WAS THE FIRST TIME THE METAL LEGENDS HAD BEEN ON THE ROAD IN 20 YEARS.

JUST ABOUT TO GO ON STAGE AT THE 1998 OZZFEST, DIME SHARES A LAUGH WITH BIG VAL, WHO WORKED SECURITY.

THE FOLLOWING YEAR, VINNIE AND DARRELL WERE PERSONALLY INVITED BY SHARON TO ATTEND OZZY'S 50TH BIRTHDAY PARTY AT THE BEVERLY SUNSET HOTEL IN LOS ANGELES.

"I DON'T KNOW ANYONE WHO WAS AS NATURAL AS HE WAS WITH PEOPLE, WITH FANS.... THAT'S WHAT MADE HIM WANT TO WAKE UP EVERY DAY AND BE PART OF THE WORLD."

—RITA HANEY, DARRELL'S GIRLFRIEND

Pantera fans came in all sizes, all ages, and from all over the world. When the original generation of Pantera fans grew up, they passed on their passion to their offspring and loved ones. Here, Darrell greets some of his young fans in Russia.

THIS FAN HAD A SPECIAL T-SHIRT MADE UP TO HUMOROUSLY EXPRESS THE EXTENT TO WHICH DIMEBAG DARRELL ABBOTT HAD AFFECTED HIS LIFE. DIME GOT A BIG KICK OUT OF IT.

SO MANY FANS JAMMED THIS RELEASE PARTY FOR *REINVENTING THE STEEL* AT TOWER RECORDS IN DALLAS THAT THE POLICE HAD TO SHUT IT DOWN ABOUT HALF-WAY THROUGH THE EVENT.

IN A MUSICAL GENRE KNOWN FOR THE TIGHT BOND BETWEEN AUDIENCE AND BAND, DARRELL AND VINNIE ABBOTT WERE PAR-TICULARLY REVERED BY METALHEADS. THEIR DOWN-HOME WAYS AND APPROACH-ABLE MANNER MADE THEM HEROES AMONG THE FANS.

Monsters of Rock

Pantera became a part of world history in September 1991 when they played the Monsters of Rock gig at Tushino Airfield in Moscow. It marked only the second time in Russian history that western heavy-metal acts performed in the still-Communist country, and it came just a month after an aborted coup. The old Soviet Union had been in the midst of reform, including economic restructuring and a loosening up of social control when the last of the hard-line Communists tried to return the country to the old ways. Anxious for reform, young Russians repelled the coup at great risk to their lives and safety. The one-day Monsters of Rock concert was billed as a celebration of democracy and freedom. Four months after the concert, the old communist Soviet Union was disbanded, and a new democratic Russia was born.

THE COWBOYS FROM HELL BRING A TASTE OF AMERICA TO THE KREMLIN.

DIME AND PANTERA'S PERFORMANCE AT THIS HISTORIC EVENT EPITOMIZED THE BEST OF HEAVY METAL.

DIME TAKES A TURN AT A BALALAIKA,
THE TRADITIONAL THREE-STRING
RUSSIAN INSTRUMENT.

MUSIC
IS
THE
UNIVERSAL
LANGUAGE.
HERE, ON THE STREETS
OF MOSCOW—WHERE
THE RUSSIAN PEOPLE
HAD JUST REPELLED
THE HARD-LINE
COMMUNISTS—DIME
AND A FAN PROVE THAT
POINT.

THE PARTY'S BACKSTAGE!

DIME STOPS THE PARTY LONG ENOUGH TO TAKE A PHOTO WITH JEFF HANNEMAN OF SLAYER, WHO HAS SWIPED VINNIE'S TRADEMARK COWBOY HAT.

PANTERA

V·I·P

VULGAR DISPLAY OF TOURING

DIME AND SCOTT IAN OF ANTHRAX CRACK UP OVER DIME'S COSTUME WHILE BACKSTAGE IN WHEELING, WEST VIRGINIA, IN 1996. ANTHRAX OPENED FOR PANTERA ON THAT TOUR, BUT THIS NIGHT, THEY LET SEBASTIAN BACH'S SOLO BAND OPEN. BACH'S GUITAR PLAYER WAS "JIMMY THE WINGMAN," AND FOR A JOKE, DIME BORROWED HIS COSTUME.

MATT SORUM, DRUMMER FOR GUNS N' ROSES AND LATER VELVET REVOLVER, PARTIES WITH DIME AND VINNIE.

ON THE ROAD, DIME WAS NOT SO
MUCH THE LIFE OF THE PARTY—
HE WAS THE PARTY.

Somewhere on the road, far from home, Dime mesmerizes the audience with his riffs and his showmanship. According to Vinnie, the European fans were among the best metalheads in the world because they lived and breathed metal.

A 1992 touring book reveals the grueling schedule of a European tour—six countries, sixteen cities, and seventeen shows in just twenty-four days.

VULGAR DISPLAY OF TOURING
EUROPE 1992

SEPTEMBER

FRI..... 11 .. DAY OFF
SAT .... 12 .. ARENA SPETTACOLI .... REGGIO EMILIA, ITALY 1
SUN ... 13 .. DAY OFF .... REGGIO EMILIA, ITALY ... 2
MON .. 14 .. PLAZA DE TOROS .... BARCELONA, SPAIN ... 3
TUE ... 15 .. VELODROMO DE ANOETA .... BARCELONA, SPAIN ... 4
WED .. 16 .. DAY OFF .... SAN SABASTIAN, SPAIN ... 5
THU ... 17 .. RECINTO HIPICO DE CACERES .... CACERES, SPAIN ... 6
FRI..... 18 .. PLAZA DE TOROS DE LAS VENTAS .... CACERES, SPAIN ... 7
SAT .... 19 .. CIRCUIT PAUL RICHARD .... MADRID, SPAIN ... 8
SUN ... 20 .. LE PHOENIX .... LE CASTELLET, FRANCE ... 9
MON .. 21 .. DAY OFF .... MULHOUSE, FRANCE .. 10
TUE ... 22 .. THE ZENITH .... PARIS, FRANCE .. 11
WED .. 23 .. DAY OFF .... PARIS, FRANCE .. 12
THU ... 24 .. ULSTER HALL .... BELFAST, IRELAND .. 13
FRI..... 25 .. POINT THEATRE .... BELFAST, IRELAND .. 14
SAT .... 26 .. DAY OFF .... DUBLIN, IRELAND .. 15
SUN ... 27 .. BIRMINGHAM INT'L ARENA .... BIRMINGHAM, ENGLAND .. 16
MON .. 28 .. PLYMOUTH PAVILIONS .... BIRMINGHAM, ENGLAND .. 17
TUE ... 29 .. HAMMERSMITH ODEON .... PLYMOUTH, ENGLAND .. 18
WED .. 30 .. HAMMERSMITH ODEON .... LONDON, ENGLAND .. 19
	LONDON, ENGLAND .. 20

OCTOBER

THU .... 1 .. NEWPORT CENTRE ....
FRI...... 2 .. DAY OFF .... NEWPORT, ENGLAND .. 21
SAT ..... 3 .. GLASGOW BARROWLAND .... GLASOW, SCOTLAND .. 22
SUN .... 4 .. CITY HALL .... GLASOW, SCOTLAND .. 23
	NEWCASTLE, ENGLAND .. 24

THOUGH THERE WAS SELDOM TIME TO TAKE IN THE SIGHTS OF EUROPE WHILE ON TOUR, DIME AND VINNIE DID VENTURE OUT WHILE IN HOLLAND IN 2000.

IN VINNIE'S WORDS
"10 More Days Till the U.S.A."

Sitting on his bus, waiting to hit the stage with his new band, Hellyeah, Vinnie Paul smiles as he remembers his brother's antics on the Far Beyond Driven tour, which was Pantera's longest and most grueling trek.

"That year we did **297 SHOWS**. We spent three months in the dead of winter in Europe on a headline tour, and we were **FUCKIN' MISERABLE**.... we're down to two weeks left. The food sucks, the weather sucks. What will we do. Then Dime comes up with '10 More Days till the U.S.A.' And just starts singin' this song. Every fuckin' day after that, '9 more days till the U.S.A. Tired of livin' this damned Euro way.' All of sudden, people are **WRITIN' ON THEIR SHOES**, '9 more days till the U.S.A.' That kind of **FUN** that would keep the whole thing from fallin' apart. He was the **KING OF IT**."

KEEPING IN TOUCH!

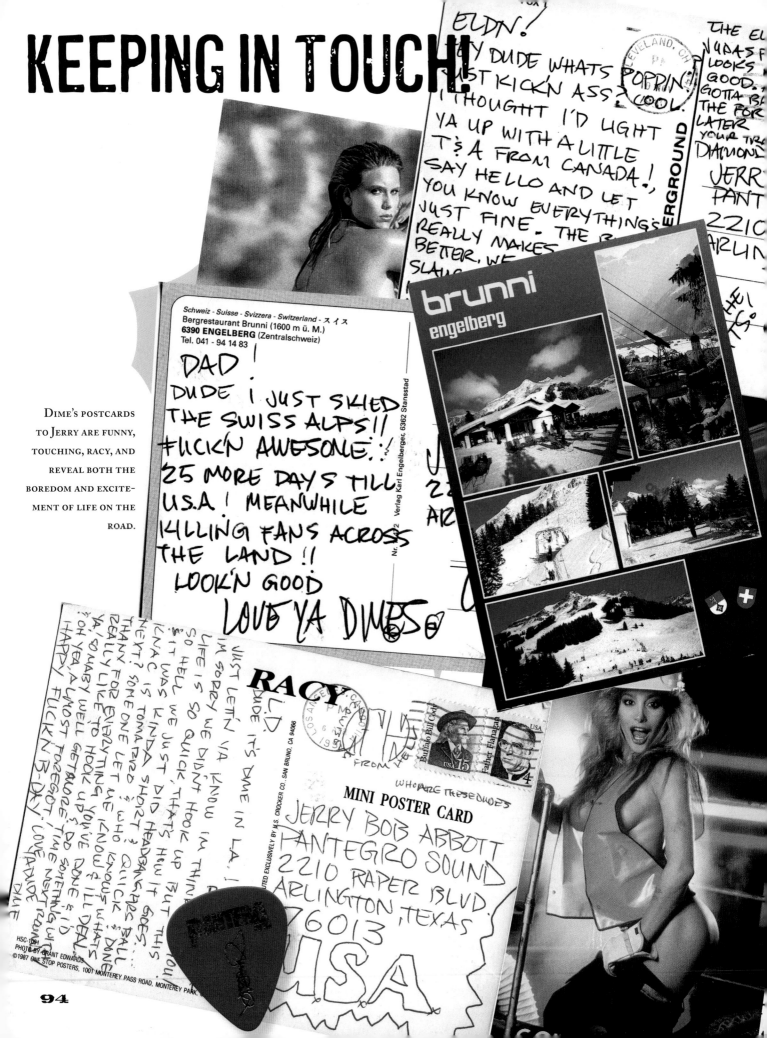

DIME'S POSTCARDS TO JERRY ARE FUNNY, TOUCHING, RACY, AND REVEAL BOTH THE BOREDOM AND EXCITEMENT OF LIFE ON THE ROAD.

ELDN!
HEY DUDE WHATS
JUST KICK'N ASS?
I THOUGHT I'D LIGHT
YA UP WITH A LITTLE
T'S A FROM CANADA!
SAY HELLO AND LET
YOU KNOW EVERYTHING'S
JUST FINE - THE B
REALLY MAKES
BETTER, WE
SLAU

CLEVELAND, CH
POPPIN'
COOL.

THE EL
NUPAS
LOOKS
GOOD.
GOTTA B
THE FOR
LATER
YOUR TR
DIAMOND
JERR
PANT
2210
ARLIN

HE!
SO
TS

Schweiz - Suisse - Svizzera - Switzerland - スイス
Bergrestaurant Brunni (1600 m ü. M.)
6390 ENGELBERG (Zentralschweiz)
Tel. 041 - 94 14 83

DAD!
DUDE I JUST SKIED
THE SWISS ALPS!!
#IICK'N AWESOME!!
25 MORE DAYS TILL
U.S.A! MEANWHILE
KILLING FANS ACROSS
THE LAND!!
LOOK'N GOOD
LOVE YA DIMES◎

brunni
engelberg

Verlag Karl Engelberger, 6362 Stanstad   Nr. 192

VJUST LET'N YA KNOW
IM SORRY WE DIDN'T
LIFE IS SO QUICK, THAT'S
OH HELL WE JUST DID
KNAC IS TOMA RVED
NEXT? SOME ONE LET
THANX FOR EVERYTHING
REALLY LIKE TO HOOK UP
YA! O MAYBY WELL GET
OH YEA, ALMOST FORGOT
HAPPY FUCK'N B-DAY!

DUDE IT'S DIME IN L.A.!
I KNOW IM THIN
HOOK UP WHATS
KINDA SHORT ?
HEADBANGERS BALL
ME WHO KNOWS WHATS
YOU'VE DONE
YOU & I'LL DEAL
MORE? DO SOMETHING UP
TIME, NEXT ROUND
LOVE DIME!
DIME!

RACY

L.A.
FROM YO

LOS ANGELES CA
PM
6
1991

Buffalo Bill Cody   Father Flanagan
USA 15   USA 4

WHO ARE THESE DUDES

MINI POSTER CARD

JERRY BOB ABBOTT
PANTEGRO SOUND
2210 RAPER BLVD
ARLINGTON, TEXAS
76013
USA

HSC-1091
PHOTO BY GRANT EDWARDS
©1987 ONE STOP POSTERS, 1001 MONTEREY PASS ROAD, MONTEREY PARK

94

...DEAN?
...DE SHIT IS VERY
WIERD. GET IT?
ANYWAY HELLO
FROM SO, SO, FAR
AWAY. CHECK
YA SOON.

...PEAN TOUR WITH
...HOLD/
...NG SON!

...3BOTT
...SOUND
...PER BLVD.
...N TEXAS
...013

25 USA

JERRY B
2310 R
ARLIN
7

LOVE

LONDON BUS

'S UP
TH CAROLINA

UP WITH THIS
S ALL RIGHT.
BEEN GOIN COOL.

JERRY BOB
2210 RAPER BLVD
ARLINGTON TEXAS
76013
U.S.A.

SURE HOPE SO.... HA HA!! LATER

IT'S GONNA PAY OFF...

In Rita's Words

Rita Haney, Darrell's longtime girl-friend, talks to you as though she has known you her whole life. Sincere, warm, and genuinely friendly, she is more than happy to talk about the man who was her best friend and the love of her life. She talks openly about the hardships of being on the road, but the time apart did not seem to hurt their relationship, because Dime was a thoughtful partner. Rita giggles and remembers the Cowboys from Hell tour:

"They **COULDN'T AFFORD TO BUY NOTHING**. And, whatever cheap hotel they were at, **DIME** would get me **SOAPS** and bottles of **SHAMPOO**. But, he would draw on them. . . . He would put this whole package together and **WRITE ME POSTCARDS** and draw **REALLY DIRTY STUFF** on the cards. He would write me letters that would go on for three or four days. They would be on toilet paper or just the back of some menu. He would com-pile them together and then **SEND ME STUFF**—make me a little **CARE PACK-AGE**. I loved all that stuff."

95

DIME TIME
Texas, Sweet Texas

A fter each grueling trek on the road, Darrell and Vinnie headed for home to recuperate, unwind, and then prepare for the next tour. For his entire life, Darrell's home—and heart—was in Arlington, Texas, the city where he was born and raised. With a population of 365,000, suburban Arlington would not seem to offer much to a heavy metal hero who had sold millions of records, been featured on the cover of virtually every

ABOVE: A HOMETOWN BOY THROUGH AND THROUGH, DIME ENJOYS A NIGHT OUT AT COWBOYS IN ARLINGTON, CIRCA 1996. RIGHT: DIME'S SERIOUS EXPRESSION AND TRADEMARK LOOK—LONG HAIR, PURPLE BEARD, AND MULTIPLE TATTOOS— BELIE A GENTLE SOUL WITH A HEART AS BIG AS TEXAS.

CHAPTER 6

hard-rock magazine in existence, and performed for millions all over the world. It isn't a cultural or artistic center, and it is far from the music industry capitals of L.A., New York, or even Nashville. Indeed, its claim to fame is its relationship to two other cities: Located halfway between Dallas and Fort Worth, it is known as the country's largest mid-city. But to Darrell and Vinnie, it was the most important city on the planet. Their attachment to Arlington proved more than a cliché about hometown boys making good; it reveals how these roots defined their personalities and their approach to their careers.

If Arlington was the one and only destination worthy of Dime Time—a term Darrell used for the rest and relaxation he needed between extended tours—the center of all activities related to this goal was his house in the Dalworthington Gardens neighborhood. The chic-sounding name for this neck of the woods is actually a clever combination of syllables from the names of the nearby anchor cities: "Dal" comes from Dallas; "worth" from Fort Worth, and "ington" is the suffix of Arlington. Like Dimebag Darrell himself, Dal-worth-ington is Texas through and through—from one end to the other.

Some architects claim that architecture can be viewed as autobiography—that is, a house and its décor not only sum up a person's external life but also reveal his personality. Darrell's house provides

RELAXING AT HOME IN ARLINGTON BETWEEN TOURS, DARRELL DECIDES TO GO BOWLING—AN UNEXPECTED PASTIME FOR A HEAVY METAL GUITAR GOD. AS JERRY IS FOND OF SAYING, "DIME WAS ALWAYS A KID; HE NEVER HAD TO GROW UP LIKE THE REST OF US."

DIME'S HOUSE WAS ALWAYS FILLED WITH SOUVENIRS, ODDITIES, AND MEMENTOES THAT REVEALED HIS UNIQUE CHARACTER. BUT AT CHRISTMAS, THERE WERE SO MANY PACKAGES AND DECORATIONS, ON TOP OF HIS OTHER CURIOS, THAT HE HUNG HIS CHRISTMAS TREE FROM THE CEILING!

a perfect example of this axiom. His home is filled with memorabilia from his career, curious mementos he collected on the road that held great meaning for him, and an array of inexplicable oddities that represent a life lived large and full. From the Damageplan poster in the hallway to the KISS memorabilia in the living room to the rolling barbed wire along the top of the walls in the den, the décor defies description. Yet it instantly reveals the man who resided there: He was a musician with an intense passion for his career, a man of great creativity and imagination, and a son of Texas who reveled in his unusual surroundings but was uninterested in material gain.

Perhaps the most striking characteristic of the house is the many items drilled to the wall. Dime loved to hang, drill, nail, or otherwise attach mementos to the wall, especially in the den, and every curio had a story. During parties, visitors tended to lose something or give something to Dime, and he dutifully drilled it to the wall. Among the most notable objects is a pair of shoes that once belonged to Robin Zander of Cheap Trick. Zander had loaned them to Dime during a concert, and Darrell kept the

shoes, commemorating the bond by drilling the shoes to the wall. The shoes are surpassed only by the mangled stop sign that hangs on the wall in the den—the result of a wayward night spent with partner in crime, Zakk Wylde. After a long evening of partying at Dime's house, the pair jumped into a friend's car and took off. Their joy ride around the neighborhood came to a screeching halt—appropriately enough—when they ran over a stop sign. Shortly thereafter, someone retrieved the sign for Dime, who thought the event should be remembered. Instead of snapping a photo, he bolted the sign to the wall—Dime's version of a souvenir.

Darrell had always wanted a jam room, where no one would bother him while he practiced or worked on new riffs for future recordings. He turned an old barn on the property into his work space, instructing the contractors to build three layers of wall in order to thoroughly soundproof it. He and Vinnie did a bit of demo recording there, and the sound was so good, Darrell decided to turn it into a working studio. Pantera's last few albums and Damageplan's *New Found Power* were all recorded there. In pure Dime fashion, the studio was not the only room that proved inspiring. Like any artist, he could be motivated anywhere, anytime—even in the bathroom. He kept a tape recorder and notebook in the bathroom, and it was not unusual for Dime to be in there with a guitar, so that whenever he was struck by a creative urge, he could get it down.

Darrell shared his life and his home in Dalworthington Gardens with his long-time girlfriend, Rita Haney. Also raised in Arlington, Rita first met Darrell when she pushed him off his bicycle in the third grade. As teenagers, the pair became close friends, bonded by a common background and common interests—particularly a passion for heavy metal music. Both had their walls plastered with posters of their idols, including KISS; both frequented the same clubs and parties, though Darrell was

"DIME WAS PROBABLY THE MOST ENTERTAINING PERSON I KNEW; HE COULD ALWAYS MAKE ME LAUGH, AND WHEN I WAS AROUND HIM, I DIDN'T WANT TO BE ANYWHERE ELSE."

—RITA HANEY, INTERVIEW, 2007

often performing while Rita was in the audience. One night after leaving the night club Savvy's, Darrell kissed Rita, which took them both by surprise. They were about 18 or 19 years old and had been friends for a long time, but they seemed ready to redefine the nature of their relationship. Shortly thereafter, they attended a Malice concert together, and later they met up with mutual friends. Dime saw one of them give Rita a friendly hug, but that did not sit well with him. Later, he called her at home and told her that he did not want her to see anyone else, and she confessed that she felt the same way.

Dime and Rita were together from that moment onward—a match made in metal music. Over the next 20 years, she was his biggest fan, his partner in fun and mischief, and someone he could trust to help handle merchandising and other business interests. Though Dime was a genius at putting together his own musical rigs to create the sounds he wanted, he cared little about computers, fax machines, and other business-related equipment. He often said, "If it ain't got six strings on it, keep it away from me." He was completely focused on his music most of the time—it moved him, fueled his creativity, and drove him to be one of the best guitar players in the world—and Rita's emotional and practical support allowed him to explore that focus without getting distracted by the details of business or everyday life.

Darrell's imagination was driven by music, but he did pursue one other creative outlet—

videography. From the time he was a teenager, he loved to shoot video of friends and family. It was also a good hobby to relieve the boredom of the road. Dime's videos had a certain style that reflected his drive and nonstop energy. He preferred fast-

DIME BECAME INTERESTED IN SHOOTING VIDEO WHILE STILL A YOUNG GUITAR SLINGER TO HELP ALLEVIATE THE BOREDOM UNTIL IT WAS TIME TO GO ON STAGE. FRIENDS AND FAMILY ATTEST TO HIS NATURAL TALENT AT VIDEOGRAPHY, NOTING HIS EYE FOR COMPOSITION AND DETAIL—WHICH THEY REFER TO AS "DIMEVISION."

paced videos that were action packed, with no lulls. And he liked to "cast" bandmates, pals, and family members in these onscreen adventures, shooting them from odd angles and at inopportune times. Dime had a lot of fun shooting video, which he often did to entertain his friends. His interest in videography spilled over into his professional life via the videos that were produced for Pantera's music. He often helped in the selection of the director and offered his perspective on the editing.

Each time Darrell and Vinnie returned home from the road, they enjoyed visiting their favorite bars, restaurants, and old haunts—including The Clubhouse, their very own strip club. In many ways, they gave back to Arlington by supporting hometown establishments, teams, and bands.

In 1999, Vinnie and Darrell composed the fight song for the Dallas Stars hockey team dubbed "Puck You," or alternately "The Dallas Stars Fight Song." Vinnie had become an avid fan of the sport, drawn to its speed, intensity, and brutality—not unlike the characteristics of his drumming style. He was also friends with team member Craig Ludwig. While playing golf one day, Ludwig suggested he compose a fight song for the team. That afternoon, Vinnie, Dime, guitar technician Grady Champion, and security director Chris Kinzy put the song together in about 90 minutes, and Vinnie dropped off the tape in Ludwig's mailbox. Vinnie heard nothing about the song until he walked into the Stars' Reunion Arena and found the team skating to it as they warmed up. The song is still played at Stars games at their new home in the American Airlines Center when the team hits the ice after every intermission.

After the Stars won the Stanley Cup in 1999, Vinnie hosted a party for the players at his house in Arlington. Because the team felt that the fight song had contributed to their winning season, they brought the Stanley Cup to Vinnie's house so that he and Dime could see it. At some point in the festivities, player Guy Carbonneau thought it would be great fun to throw the Cup off the balcony into the pool. Unfortunately, the aim was not true, and the Cup hit the side of the pool before it landed in the water, resulting in a major dent in the bottom of the century-old trophy. There was a brief uproar about the damage, but eventually the Cup was fixed.

DARRELL IS ANOINTED BY DEFENSE PLAYER RICHARD MATVICHUK FROM THE STANLEY CUP AS HE HELPS THE DALLAS STARS CELEBRATE THEIR FIRST CHAMPIONSHIP. DEFENSEMAN CRAIG LUDWIG (IN RED) CHEERS DIME ON.

Another way the Abbott brothers kept in touch with their Arlington roots was to perform every New Year's Eve at local clubs. With Pantera on hiatus during the Christmas holidays, Vinnie and Dime formed a loose-knit group with Thurber T. Mingus and Sean Time, members of a local band called Pumpjack. They called the band Gasoline, which performed only in Arlington on New Year's Eve. Each year the venue was different and generally small, but one holiday, they opened for Drowning Pool before a crowd of 3000.

Dime was always aware of the importance of giving back to his community in any number of ways. He not only supported local bands by offering his guidance or connections, but he also came to the rescue of musicians in need of equipment. He liked being part of Arlington, and residents were genuinely fond of its most colorful resident. Many Arlington natives still tell Dime stories that testify to his larger-than-life yet down-to-earth personality—a rare combination. Such is a story told by Cowboy Cunningham, who at the time worked security at The Clubhouse. One Christmas Eve, he stopped by the local Walmart about 3 a.m. for some last-minute Christmas shopping. He was stunned to see Dime and Rita riding around the store on a Rascal scooter—the motorized cart generally available for seniors unable to withstand the rigors of shopping on foot. "Dime," he shouts, "What are you doin' on that thing?" "Christmas shoppin', man, whaddya think," Darrell calls back, and with a wave, he and Rita disappeared into the aisles of the Walmart.

"DIME WAS ONE OF THOSE PEOPLE WHO DIDN'T CONFORM, BUT YOU COULD STILL RELATE TO HIM."

—JERRY ABBOTT, INTERVIEW, 2007

This unique sculpture, which stands just outside the front door of Darrell's home in Dalworthington Gardens, captures the essence of Dime by echoing his trademark look and including symbols associated with him, such as the razor blade and his Dean guitar.

The walls of the entranceway and game room are lined with personal photos that held great meaning for Darrell. The game room contains pinball machines, a pool table, and the jukebox that Vinnie gave Dime for Christmas one year.

TOP AND MIDDLE: GOLD RECORDS, POSTERS, AND OTHER MEMENTOES NOT ONLY CHRONICLE DARRELL'S CAREER BUT ALSO ATTEST TO THE SUCCESS OF PANTERA AND DAMAGEPLAN. BOTTOM: VINNIE, DIME, AND TEXAS COMEDIAN THE CHINAMAN CELEBRATE THE LATTER'S BIRTHDAY IN 2004.

DIMEbonics

Dime had his own language, which he dubbed Dimebonics, with an offbeat turn of phrase for all occasions. If you could figure out what he was saying the first time around, then you were on his wavelength.

GETCHA PULL To get in on the action, or join in; be a part of the party, have a drink, enjoy yourself.

WIG Hair

PIPES Singing voice

RIG OR COSTUME Clothes

LARD OUT Rest at home, doing very little

GENE SIMMONS BEAUTY REST His personal bed

THAT'S CASUAL That's okay, that's cool

LET'S LIGHT IT UP Let's get something going; let's do it

CADILLAC ROCK BOX Dime's Escalade SUV

PARTY WITH DIME!

DARRELL'S REPUTATION AS THE LIFE
OF THE PARTY BEGAN EARLY.

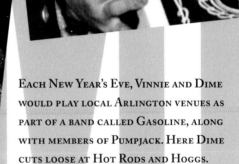

EACH NEW YEAR'S EVE, VINNIE AND DIME
WOULD PLAY LOCAL ARLINGTON VENUES AS
PART OF A BAND CALLED GASOLINE, ALONG
WITH MEMBERS OF PUMPJACK. HERE DIME
CUTS LOOSE AT HOT RODS AND HOGGS.

Dime Destination
The Clubhouse

In 1996, according to *Texas Monthly* magazine, **VINNIE** and **DIME** became participating partners in an **ADULT NIGHT CLUB** on Manana Drive in Dallas. They dubbed it **THE CLUBHOUSE**, because they had originally intended it to be part of a rock 'n' roll-themed golf course with a strip club at the 19th hole. Though the golf course part of the plan proved too impractical to construct, the **GOLF THEME** remained via the decor of the club, which includes lithographs of famous golfers and courses. It is also the home of several of **DIME'S DEAN GUITARS**, which he gave to the Club, in addition to tons of rock 'n' roll **MEMORABILIA** and **GOLD AND PLATINUM RECORDS** donated by countless rock stars that have downed a shot at The Clubhouse. Dime and Vinnie sometimes held album-release parties there, or simply relaxed among friends. They also entertained celebrity guests such as **KISS** and **BLACK SABBATH** as well as athletes from Dallas's sport teams and NASCAR drivers. The Clubhouse quickly became a successful local attraction. As Vinnie told *Texas Monthly*, " . . . where else in the country are you virtually guaranteed to see **ROCK STARS** and **NAKED WOMEN** almost every night? Only at 'The Clubhouse' in Texas."

Each Halloween, the Abbotts hosted a costume party, usually at Vinnie's. In 2002, Darrell (second from left) came as David Allan Coe, while Vinnie dressed up as "the ghost of Vinnie Paul." Friends Sterling Winfield (left) and Pete High (right) join the festivities.

In 1998, Darrell hosted the Halloween party. His costume is based on the character Powder from the film of the same name.

For this party, Darrell came as an alien, while Sterling Winfield seemed content to bat his extra-long lashes.

Dime's Bar

BLACK TOOTH GRIN

1 SHOT SEAGRAM'S 7
SPLASH OF DIET COKE

CROWN TOOTH GRIN

1 SHOT CROWN ROYAL
SPLASH OF DIET COKE

WHITE TOOTH GRIN

1 SHOT VODKA
SPLASH OF WATER

All can be served chilled or at room temperature.

A Tour of Dime's Den

When Dime first bought his house, Vinnie was a bit taken aback because the inside was decorated with a dull, conventional baby-blue wallpaper—something a senior citizen might choose. Vinnie need not have worried, because even before the official papers were all signed, Dime had begun to customize the house to reflect his thoroughly unique tastes and one-of-a-kind personality. Of all the rooms in the house, the den most captures his spirit. The rolling barbed wire along the top of the ceiling, the wagon-wheel chandelier, and the corrugated tin on the walls are an homage to his Texas roots. The dolls and statues in Dime's likeness are reminders of his star image as "Dimebag Darrell," while the stop sign and shoes drilled to the wall are mementos of fun times with such friends as Zakk Wylde and Robin Zander. So, sit back, peruse the photos, and "getcha pull."

DIME'S
FAVORITE TV SHOWS

UNSOLVED MYSTERIES

THE NEW DETECTIVES

COLD CASE FILES

FORENSIC FILES

RITA AND DIME

When Darrell began calling himself Dimebag, he dubbed Rita "Dimebag's Hag." They affectionately referred to themselves as "the Bag and his Hag."

Dime (red t-shirt) and Rita (third from right) grew up together as friends, which gave them a common background. Rita recalls feeling protective toward him when they were kids, often sticking up for him when he was picked on. Still protective, she works to ensure that his music and memory will stay alive.

Rita

Born in 1966 in McKinney, Texas, **RITA SUE HANEY** was raised in Arlington. She **MET** Darrell when the two were **IN THE THIRD GRADE** at Beatrice Short Elementary School, though she did not really like him at first. Sensing that Darrell was more imaginative and funny than most boys, Rita soon changed her mind. The two had **MUCH IN COMMON**: Rita's aunt lived on Darrell's block; both of their mothers worked; they were born within days of each other; and they loved music. They went to their first concert together at age 11—to see KISS, of course.

They lost touch for a few years during their early teens, because Rita lived on the other side of town. After Pantera began to play at local venues, she went to see them play, and she and Darrell resumed their friendship. An odd non-romance existed between them for a few years, with Rita often introducing Darrell to girls who wanted to get to know him. Eventually, the two realized there was more to the relationship than friendship, and Rita became a **MAJOR PART OF DIME'S LIFE**.

After Darrell bought his house, Rita moved in to take care of it while he was on tour. She also took care of many of his business interests and never wavered in **HER SUPPORT** of his music. Their **LONG-LASTING RELATIONSHIP** was an anomaly in the world of rock 'n' roll and respected by their friends and associates. Tom Maxwell, formerly of Nothingface and currently a member of Hellyeah, recalled a conversation he had with Dime about Rita in which Darrell confessed, "I pride myself on knowing I am dedicated to her."

AN UNCONVENTIONAL PAIR, the two decided that marriage and children were not for them, but they were absolutely devoted to each other. As Rita once declared, "I had a lot of Dime time. And I am fortunate for that. We had 20 years, and that's more than most people get who are married."

RITA WITNESSED DIME'S CAREER FROM THE BEGINNING AND CHRONICLED IT WITH SNAP-SHOTS. THOUGH THE PHOTOS ARE OLD AND FADED, THEY OFFER AN INTIMATE PORTRAIT OF A LEGEND IN THE MAKING, AS CAPTURED BY THE WOMAN WHO KNEW HIM BEST.

Dime Time in Memphis

One year, Vinnie and Darrell joined their father Jerry—affectionately known as L.D.—in Memphis for his birthday. L.D. wanted the boys to get in touch with the roots of their music, so he introduced them to such pioneers as Elvis Presley, Jerry Lee Lewis, and the performers who had been part of Stax Records. Jerry had moved to Nashville to produce country music after Pantera signed with a nationally based management company, and the Memphis vacation became a way for the family to reconnect. Going to Memphis became a family tradition, which Jerry and Vinnie still do.

DIME, L.D., AND VINNIE SOAK UP THE VIBES IN THE LEGENDARY SUN STUDIO, WHERE ELVIS, JERRY LEE LEWIS, CARL PERKINS, JOHNNY CASH, ROY ORBISON, AND MANY OTHER ROCKABILLY LEGENDS GOT THEIR START.

AT SUN STUDIO, DIME AND VINNIE ARE RECOGNIZED BY THE TOUR GUIDE, PLANET, WHO IS THE DAUGHTER OF ROCK 'N' ROLLER BILLY SWAN.

WHEN EATING AT THE SUN STUDIO CAFE (FORMERLY THE TAYLOR CAFE), VISITORS ARE SURROUNDED BY THE MUSICAL HISTORY OF SAM PHILLIPS' LEGENDARY RECORDING STUDIO. MOST OF THE PIONEERS WHO RECORDED AT SUN ENDED UP EATING AT THIS TINY CAFE. TABLE #1, WHERE DIME AND VINNIE ARE SITTING, WAS OFTEN OCCUPIED BY ELVIS PRESLEY HIMSELF.

DIMEBAG DARRELL STANDS ON THE PORCH OF GRACE-LAND, ELVIS'S HOME IN MEMPHIS. PRIOR TO VISITING MEMPHIS WITH JERRY, DIME AND VINNIE KNEW EL-VIS ONLY THROUGH THE CHRISTMAS RECORDS THEIR MOTHER HAD PLAYED ON HOLIDAYS. WHILE WALKING THE GROUNDS OF GRACELAND, THEY LEARNED OF ELVIS'S IMPACT AS A PERFORMER. THEY WERE PARTICULARLY IMPRESSED WITH THE FACT THAT ELVIS SOLD OVER 400 MILLION RECORDS WITHOUT LEAVING THE U.S.A., SAVE FOR A BRIEF TOUR OF CANADA DURING THE 1950S.

VINNIE AND DARRELL CHECK OUT ELVIS'S GOLD AND PLATINUM RECORDS AS WELL AS HIS JUMPSUITS AND VIDEOS ON DISPLAY IN THE RAQUETBALL COURT.

L.D. AND DIME CHECK OUT ELVIS'S PRIVATE PLANE NAMED AFTER HIS DAUGHTER, LISA MARIE.

L.D., Vinnie, and Dime enjoyed the sites and sounds of Memphis's legendary Beale Street.

WHILE STROLLING OUTSIDE THE RUM BOOGIE CAFÉ, DIME WAS RECOGNIZED BY ONE OF THE CAFÉ'S EMPLOYEES. THE YOUNG MAN RAN OUTSIDE AND STOPPED DARRELL TO ASK HIM TO AUTOGRAPH ONE OF THE GUITARS HANGING FROM THE WALLS AND CEILING OF THE RESTAURANT. DIME AND VINNIE BOTH SIGNED THE GUITAR, WHICH STILL HANGS NEAR THE FRONT OF THE CAFÉ.

50th ANNIVERSARY
SUN Studio
ADMIT ONE
Studio Tour
The Birthplace of
Rock 'n Roll™
706 Union Ave., Memphis TN 38103
800-441-6249 • info@sunstudio.com
http://www.sunstudio.com
No. 111575

IN NESBITT, MISSISSIPPI, JUST SOUTH OF MEMPHIS, JERRY SNAPS DIME AND VINNIE IN FRONT OF THE HOUSE OF ROCKABILLY LEGEND JERRY LEE LEWIS, WHOSE NICKNAME, THE KILLER, SPEAKS TO THE FEROCITY OF HIS PIANO PLAYING.

DOIN' IT DIME STYLE

Dime commemorated significant events with tattoos; in a way, they were autobiographical. After the success of Pantera's first album for Atco, he got a *Cowboys from Hell* tattoo on his right arm; another tattoo marks the importance of the Pantera song "Domination"; "Black tooth" is written on his body in Portuguese; and on the 50th anniversary of Roswell, he got an alien tattoo. One of Dime's most personal tattoos is the face and signature of KISS guitarist Ace Frehley emblazoned on his chest.

Dime wore a razor blade around his neck as an homage to Judas Priest's album *British Steel*. Rita had the first razor blade necklace made for him at a local Arlington jeweler. The colorful beard was also inspired by Rita, who used to dye her hair purple. One day when she was coloring her hair, Dime stuck his beard in the dye, and the rest is heavy metal history.

FROM THE BEGINNING OF HIS CAREER, DIME'S
HAIR WAS AN EXPRESSIVE PART OF HIS PERSONAL-
ITY AND PERFORMANCE. ONSTAGE, HIS WILD,
SWIRLING LOCKS WERE AS DISTINCTIVE AND
RECOGNIZABLE AS HIS GUITAR SOLOS.

GUITARS
PROUD TO BE LOUD

listering. Tantalizing. Brutal. Fiery. Frenetic. Ear-shattering. Throughout Dimebag Darrell Abbott's career, journalists, fans, and guitar magazines used these adjectives and more to describe his guitar playing—a style and sound that is basically indescribable. Steeped in Texas musical traditions and then inspired by the great metal guitar slingers, Darrell absorbed these influences to become a true innovator in the art of shredding. He not

AN AD FOR A PROMINENT GUITAR MANUFACTURER READS, "LYRICS. WASTED TIME BETWEEN SOLOS"—A SLOGAN THAT COULD EASILY HAVE BEEN WRITTEN FOR DIMEBAG DARRELL. AT RIGHT, DIME MESMERIZES THE AUDIENCE WITH A SOLO ON HIS LEGENDARY DEAN FROM HELL.

only mastered the arsenal of metal techniques, he added to them.

It all began with that Hohner Les Paul copy that 11-year-old Darrell carried to Jerry's house to learn Van Halen's "Runnin' with the Devil." Solid, comfortable, and durable, the Hohner made a good starter guitar, but eventually Dime outgrew it. When he was 16, he had his sights set on a Dean guitar. Finally, after much prodding, Jerry bought him his first Dean as a Christmas gift, beginning a life-long love affair between Dime and his Deans.

But it was more than the guitars that shaped Darrell's talents. He was also influenced by the local guitar players whom he heard when they recorded at his father's studio, Pantego Sound, including Rocky Athas of Lightning, who was known for his harmonics, and bluesy performers like Bugs Henderson and Jimmy Wallace. Rock critics and historians frequently debate the exact relationship between blues and heavy metal, while many metal band members are unaware of the roots of their own music. With Dime, the connection was direct and unarguable. Blues-influenced guitar work is a part of where he came from, and it informed his own playing in subtle ways

that gave his sound depth, melody, and direction—no matter how heavy he wanted to go. Nowhere was this more apparent than in his solos. Other metal guitar slingers played for speed or for volume, but Darrell's solos were—and are—memorable because they were melodic at the core.

DARRELL CHECKS OUT THE LATEST DEAN AT AN AUDIO-VIDEO EXPO IN DALLAS.

Dime progressed rapidly as a player, and when he was still an adolescent, he began entering local guitar contests as Diamond Darrell. He was so young that his mother, Carolyn, had to drive him to the contest locations. Generally sponsored by local music stores, the contests often offered a new guitar as the top prize. According to Ricky Lynn Gregg, member of the group Savvy and an inspiration to the Abbott Brothers, he was a judge at one of the first contests Darrell entered—if not the first. The contest was held at the Agora Ballroom, a major rock 'n' roll venue in Dallas. Most of the ten contestants ranged in age between 19 and 35, except for Darrell who was around 14. Darrell was the last contestant to compete. He began with a few licks of his own and then launched into a blistering rendition of "Eruption." Gregg recalled for *Guitar World* magazine that he and the panel of judges decided Darrell was the winner even before he finished his set. "He was a maniac virtuoso, even way back then," Gregg noted.

Family members and friends take great delight in recalling how Diamond Darrell blew away the competition to win contest after contest, including the time he won a 1981 Dean ML just a few weeks after Jerry had bought him his first Dean. Though he was excited at owning two Dean guitars, Darrell was also 16 years old, and the impulse to have his own car became too much for him to resist. He decided to sell one of his guitars to raise the cash for a car. He knew how difficult it had been for his dad to come up with the money to buy the Dean he had gotten for Christmas, so Dime sold the contest guitar for $600. With the money, he bought a bright yellow 1972 Pontiac Firebird Formula. The car meant so much to him that he kept it his entire life, and it still sits on the grounds of his home in Texas.

DIME'S 1972 CLASSIC FIREBIRD FORMULA WAS FITTED WITH THE PERIOD-POPULAR REAR-WINDOW SUNSHADE, CRAGAR SS MAG WHEELS, AND WIDE REAR TIRES. IN THE 1970S, BRIGHT YELLOW WAS A POPULAR COLOR FOR SPORTY-LOOKING CARS.

GUITARS PROUD TO BE LOUD

"I DON'T PLAY GOLF,
I DON'T PLAY BASEBALL...
I DON'T WORK ON CARS.
THERE AIN'T NOTHING ELSE.
THERE'S MUSIC AND
THAT'S IT."

— DARRELL ABBOTT,
QUOTED IN GREAT FALLS TRIBUNE, DECEMBER 10, 2004

The contest Dean ML changed hands a few times before coming into the possession of Buddy Blaze, a Texas six-string guitar master who was employed by Kramer Guitars. Blaze had the Dean custom-painted blue and then added a decorative touch that made the guitar memorable. Lightning bolts were emblazoned across the body—a symbol that evoked all that is important to a true guitar slinger. It was

electric, it was dangerous, it was primal. Later, after Blaze returned the Dean to Darrell, a grateful Dime dubbed it "the Dean from Hell."

Darrell not only had a history with Dean guitars, he also fostered a friendship with Dean Zelinsky—designer of the fabled guitar and founder of the company. Zelinsky had already heard of Diamond Darrell, this kid who was winning all of the Dean-sponsored contests in the Dallas-Fort Worth area, when he headed to the Spier Music Store in Texas for a promotion during the mid-1980s. Dime decided it was time to meet Zelinsky, and he showed up at the music store with his modified Dean guitar. He plugged in a Marshall amp and then cranked it up for Zelinsky to hear. Needless to say, he made a lasting impression.

Dean and Dime got along instantly, because they spoke the same language. Zelinsky appreciated that Darrell, despite his youth, knew what he wanted in a guitar. And Dime liked Zelinsky's guitars because they were cutting edge. Dean was taking guitar design in a different direction—pointy, streamlined, and sleek—just like Dime and Pantera would push metal toward a harder, deeper edge. Other com-

DIME VISITS THE DEAN GUITARS FACTORY WITH FOUNDER DEAN
ZELINSKY.

panies' instruments were just too conservative for
the direction that Dime was headed. In addition to
the aesthetics of the design, Dime preferred the
tone of the Dean as well as its ease of playing. Its
body shape allowed for easy access to the bottom
strings, which were crucial to Dime's heavy-sound-
ing riffs and leads.

Zelinsky sold his company in 1991, but Darrell
continued to endorse Dean guitars until 1994. During the late 1990s, Dime made a deal with Washburn
guitars, though the relationship lacked the personal
touch that he had enjoyed with Dean. Zelinsky
returned to the company that he founded in 2000,
and Elliott Rubinson, the current CEO, immediately
asked Dean if they could possibly get Dimebag Darrell to endorse their product. Dime was the perfect
choice to reinvigorate Dean guitars; not only was he
metal's most admired shredder, he had a real history with the Dean.

Zelinsky signed Darrell in November 2004. The
pair's first endeavor was to re-introduce the Dean
ML, which was made available in a limited edition
of 150 and in a variety of colors. Called Dimebag
Darrell's Dean Collection, all of the guitars were
pre-sold. Two years later, Dean relaunched Dime's
favorite guitar as the Dean from Hell CFH Electric
Guitar in an accurate reproduction, complete with
the guitar slinger's preferred modifications.

Dean and Darrell's most historic creation was the
Razorback, a guitar that Dime developed himself.
With its pointed ends and hook-like barbs along
the top, the Razorback was and is the ultimate metal
weapon. Though Dime never got to see the finished
product, the guitar and its importance to heavy
metal history have become part of his legacy.

THE HISTORIC
RAZORBACK FEATURES
"DIME" PRINTED IN
BLOCK LETTERS ON THE
HEADSTOCK.

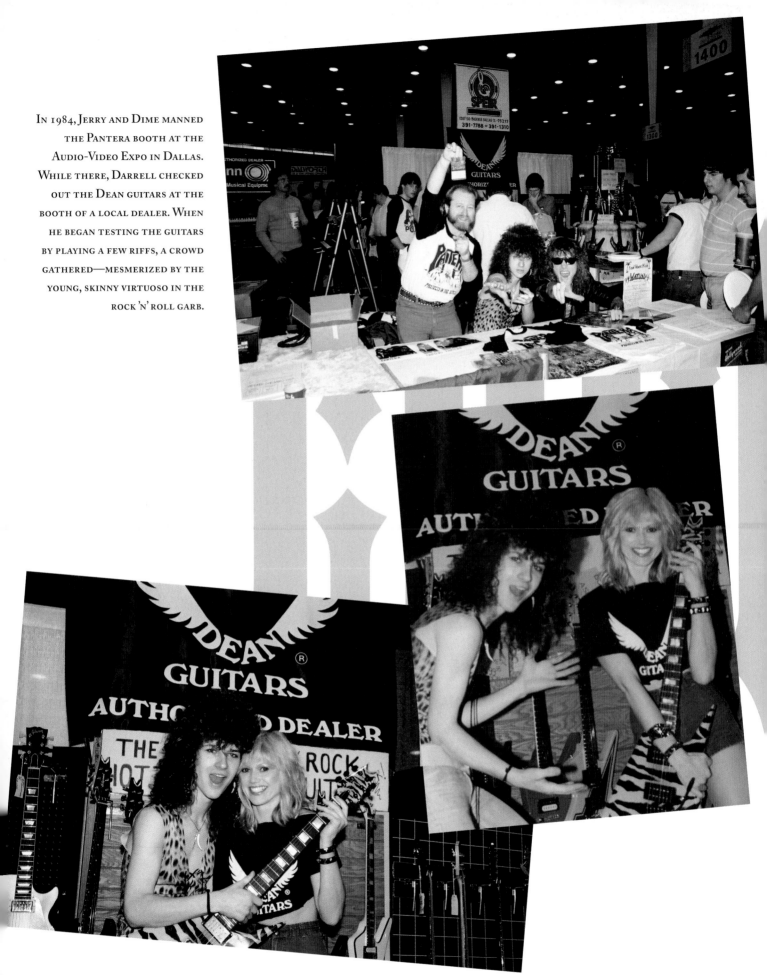

In 1984, Jerry and Dime manned the Pantera booth at the Audio-Video Expo in Dallas. While there, Darrell checked out the Dean guitars at the booth of a local dealer. When he began testing the guitars by playing a few riffs, a crowd gathered—mesmerized by the young, skinny virtuoso in the rock 'n' roll garb.

THE DEAN FROM HELL

THE FOUR FACES OF THE MEMBERS OF KISS ADORN THE AREA BEHIND THE BRIDGE ON THE FRONT OF THE DEAN FROM HELL. DIME'S ORIGINAL MUSICAL INFLUENCE— ACE FREHLEY—WAS NEVER OFF HIS RADAR.

WITH HIS PICK IN HIS MOUTH, DIME CONCENTRATES ON TAPPING OUT "ERUPTION" ON THE GUITAR THAT HE MADE FAMOUS.

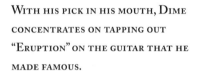

THE BACKSIDE OF THIS DEAN—WHICH WAS THE ONE GIVEN TO DIME BY L.D.—REVEALS EVIDENCE OF HIS MODIFICATIONS. HE ROUTED OUT THE BACK AND INSTALLED A FLOYD ROSE LOCKING SYSTEM AND NONSTOCK PICKUPS TO HELP ATTAIN THE SOUND HE WAS SEARCHING FOR.

THIS CUT-OUT OF DIMEBAG DARRELL IMMORTALIZES THE GUITAR SLINGER AND HIS WEAPON OF CHOICE, THE DEAN FROM HELL. DIME JOINS A LONG LINE OF GUITARISTS FROM ALL GENRES OF POPULAR MUSIC WHO WERE ASSOCIATED WITH INSTRUMENTS THAT BECAME LEGENDARY, SUCH AS BLUES MASTER B.B. KING AND "LUCILLE," EDDIE VAN HALEN AND HIS BLACK-AND-WHITE STRIPED "FRANKENSTRAT," ERIC CLAPTON'S COMPOSITE STRATOCASTER "BLACKIE," AND Z.Z. TOPS' DEAN SPINNING FUR GUITARS.

Fate

After Darrell **SOLD** the **DEAN ML** that he won in a contest in order to buy his yellow **FIREBIRD**, the guitar eventually ended up in the possession of **BUDDY BLAZE**. A true aficionado, Blaze **BUILT AND REPAIRED** guitars, so it is no surprise that he gave the ML its now legendary customized paint job. One day, Dime saw the **BRIGHT BLUE** guitar with the **LIGHTNING BOLT DESIGN** on display in the store where Blaze worked. He wanted to buy it, not realizing it was the same ML that he had sold. Buddy declined Dime's offer, but the two struck up a **FRIENDSHIP**, eventually discovering the true provenance of the ML.

Buddy had agreed to put together a customized guitar for Dime in exchange for a Gibson Flying V that Dime owned, but the busy Blaze couldn't seem to find the time. One day, he showed up at Dime's door with a box. When the young guitarist opened the box, he was shocked to see the Dean ML laying inside. Buddy said, "Dude, **IT WAS YOUR PRIZE** to begin with."

A Guitar Hero's Heroes

Dime salutes Judas Priest, a band that was not only an influence but also responsible for Pantera's first European tour. In front in black is Priest bass player Ian Hill. Standing from left are Priest drummer Scott Travis, Dime, Priest guitarist K.K. Downing, Zakk Wylde of Black Label Society, Vinnie Paul, Kerry King of Slayer, and Priest guitarist Glenn Tipton.

Dime strums an acoustic guitar autographed by players he admired, including Steve Vai, Yngwie Malmsteen, Al Di Meola, and Joe Satriani. The guitar belonged to an autograph hound who brought it along to a meet-and-greet for Dime to sign. As Dime continued to play, he broke into the theme song to *Chappelle's Show*, and everyone joined in.

Dime's own reputation as a guitar slinger ranged far and wide. Here he shows crew member Jeff Judd a guitar he had autographed for the Hard Rock Café in Mexico City.

İn Vіnnіе's Words

Vinnie recalls a **RAUCOUS** good time at the grand opening of the Hard Rock Café Vault in Orlando, Florida, when he and Dime were invited to **SHAKE THINGS UP** for the press and attendees.

"There were **MANY ROCK STARS** in attendance including Nikki Sixx of Motley Crue, Slash and Duff from Guns n' Roses, Brian Johnson of AC/DC, Zakk Wylde, and, of course, me and Dime. Don Bernstein (curator for the Hard Rock) wanted to pull a **CRAZY STUNT** on the attendees, and he knew **THE ONLY STARS** that were **CRAZY ENOUGH** to do it was **ME AND DIME**.

There was a **RED CARPET** and every [form of] **MEDIA** you can think of—from *Entertainment Tonight* to MTV to NBC, CBS, ABC, etc...**A BIG EVENT** .... Well, they were delivering the last piece of memorabilia that night, which was the first guitar ever given to the Hard Rock by Eric Clapton. Don wanted us to seem like we were **GRABBING** the guitar to **DESTROY IT** as it was being brought inside .... We took it **ONE STEP FURTHER**. We bought **LIGHTER FLUID** on the way and figured we would pull a **"HENDRIX"** on that guitar. We were the last ones dropped off via limo onto the red carpet ... and we stood with the other rockers. The Hard Rock truck pulled up and opened the back gate revealing the prize possession **[ERIC CLAPTON'S GUITAR]**. As they brought it down the walkway, we got the sign from Don to **GO FOR IT**. Dime jumped out and grabbed it, held it up in the air, and then started **SMASH-ING IT** on the ground. The crowd was **FREAKIN' OUT**, and I was **SQUIRTING LIGHTER FLUID** on it. We **LIT IT** and gave the "Hendrix Pose," [photo above]. About this time, they brought out **THE REAL GUITAR** .... Everyone **CHEERED** and sighed in relief .... Then we got wasted and Don lost his mind .... [photo above] **WHAT A GREAT NIGHT!**"

THE POSITION OF THE HANDS IN THESE PHOTOS REVEALS THAT DIME IS WORKING STRINGS 4, 5, AND 6. MOST PLAYERS LEARN TO PLAY LEADS ON STRINGS 1, 2, AND 3, AND THEN PREFER THOSE STRINGS ABOVE ALL OTHERS. BUT DIME WAS AS ADEPT AT PERFORMING SOLOS ON THE LARGER, LOWER STRINGS AS HE WAS ON THE SMALLER ONES. THE LOWER STRINGS PRODUCE A MORE POWERFUL NOTE WITH A THICKER TONE, RESULTING IN THE CRUNCHY SOUND OF HEAVY METAL. THE COMBINATION OF DIME'S PLAYING STYLE AND THE WAY HIS DEANS LAID AGAINST HIS BODY MADE HIM EXTREMELY QUICK AND DEADLY ACCURATE ON STRINGS 4, 5 AND 6. OTHER PLAYERS MARVELED AT HIS TECHNIQUE AND THE USE OF THOSE STRINGS IN HIS LEAD PLAYING.

AT AN EARLY AGE, DARRELL MASTERED A TECHNIQUE KNOWN AS TAPPING, FAMOUSLY USED BY EDDIE VAN HALEN ON "ERUPTION." IT IS A TWO-HANDED TECHNIQUE IN WHICH THE RIGHT HAND "TAPS OUT" EXTRA NOTES ON THE FRET BOARD, CREATING LICKS THAT ARE IMPOSSIBLE TO PLAY WITH JUST THE LEFT HAND. OFTEN, IT IS ACCOMPANIED BY PULL-OFFS AND HAMMER-ONS, WHICH DIME MASTERED IN HIS VERY EARLY TEENS. VAN HALEN MAY HAVE BROUGHT IT TO THE FORE FOR HARD ROCKERS AND HEAVY METAL GUITARISTS, BUT THE TECHNIQUE PRECEDED HIM BY DECADES, IF NOT CENTURIES. IT APPEARS AS EARLY AS PAGANINI'S (1782-1840) TECHNIQUES ON THE VIOLIN. IT WAS ALSO USED IN THE 1950S AND 1960S BY JAZZ GREAT BARNEY KESSEL. ROCKERS BEGAN TO PICK UP ON IT IN THE MID 1970S. PLAYERS SUCH AS ACE FREHLEY, FRANK ZAPPA, BILLY GIBBONS, BRIAN MAY, AND LESLIE WEST WERE SOME OF THE EARLIEST ROCKERS TO INCORPORATE TAPPING. VAN HALEN CITES MULTI-FACETED BRITISH JAZZ PLAYER ALLAN HOLDSWORTH AS HIS MENTOR. IN DIME'S CASE, HE HAD BEEN INFLUENCED BY LOCAL LEGEND ROCKY ATHAS, WHO WAS A MASTER.

SOME OF DIME'S HIGH-PITCHED HARMONIC SQUEALS WERE THE RESULT OF HIS WHAMMY BAR TECHNIQUE, WHICH ACCORDING TO DIME WERE ACCOMPLISHED BY FLICKING A STRING, SLAMMING THE BAR ALL THE WAY TO THE BODY OF THE GUITAR, THEN TAPPING A HARMONIC WHILE SIMULTANEOUSLY RELEASING THE WHAMMY BAR; THE RESULT WAS A FRENETICALLY CHARGED HIGH-PITCHED SQUEAL HE WOULD THEN MANIPULATE WITH FINAL QUIVERS OF THE WHAMMY BAR. DIME WAS INFLUENCED BY STEVE VAI WITH THIS TECHNIQUE, THOUGH HE TOYED WITH IT TO MAKE IT HIS OWN.

DIME TUNED HIS GUITAR DOWNWARD AS MUCH AS A TONE AND A HALF FROM THE UNIVERSAL SETTING OF A-440 IN ORDER TO GET THE MASSIVE SOUND NECESSARY FOR THE HEAVIEST OF METAL. TUNING DOWN RISKS LOSING THE CLARITY OF THE NOTES, BUT DIME'S NOTES WERE ALWAYS CLEARLY DISTINGUISHABLE.

During the mid-1990s, Dime signed with Washburn guitars. He worked closely with Washburn to come up with an instrument that revealed who he was as a guitar slinger. Called the Dimebag Darrell model, the guitar came in several finishes that were approved by Dime and reflected his tastes and identity. Among the finishes were the DimeSlime, the DimeBolt, the BlackJack—adorned with the logo for his favorite whiskey, Seagram's 7, and a limited edition Confederate flag.

In Jerry's Words
"What Kind of Gadgets Have You Got?"

Jerry lightly laughs as he brings up Dime's love of pawn shops. From haggling with the owner to discovering some guitar gadget from an old beat-up, discarded instrument, he loved to peruse the pawn shops, buy cheap gear, and apply it to his rig. Anything that might affect the sound coming from his axe was fair game.

"On the [*Vulgar Display of Power*] album, **DIME** just couldn't find the lead that he trul-wanted on the song "Regular People." **TERRY DATE** (the engineer) asked him, 'What kind of **GADGETS** have you got?' Dime said, 'You should never ask me that because I got a **MILLION OF 'EM**. I got a room full.' Dime and Terry got three or four types of gadgets, hooked them all up, and made all kinds of **TREMENDOUS NOISE**. They recorded something the rest of the band all loved. And Dime said, 'I defy anybody to ever get that sound again!'"

IN LATE 2004, DIME RE-SIGNED WITH DEAN GUITARS AND RENEWED HIS
WORKING RELATIONSHIP WITH DEAN ZELINSKY. THEY REINTRODUCED THE
DEAN ML IN VARIOUS FINISHES, DUBBING THEM DIMEBAG DARRELL'S DEAN
COLLECTION. THIS MODEL HAD ALWAYS HELD A SPECIAL MEANING FOR
ZELINSKY, BECAUSE THE INITIALS ML WERE THOSE OF ONE OF HIS BEST
FRIENDS WHO HAD LOST HIS LIFE AS A TEENAGER. AND IT WAS SPECIAL FOR
DIME BECAUSE HE HAD A STORIED HISTORY WITH HIS OLD DEAN FROM HELL.
AMONG THE FINISHES WERE THE DIME-O-FLAME (ABOVE LEFT), THE FBD
TRIBUTE (ABOVE RIGHT), AND THE DIME-O-FLAGE (RIGHT).

In 1993, *Guitar World* magazine asked Darrell to write a regular column featuring tips and advice on how to shred Dime-style. Nick Bowcott, a renowned rock-music journalist who was part of the *GW* staff, was assigned to work with Dime on his columns. Dime wrote 28 columns from the April 1993 issue to the September 1995 issue. In 2003, Bowcott released a book based on Dime's columns titled *Riffer Madness*, an informal but informative guide to Darrell's techniques and style

Dime's popularity with head-bangers was evident in the many times he graced the covers of guitar magazines during his career. The magazines detail everything from the guitar star's biography to his favorite gear to how to play his most famous leads and riffs.

Guitar and metal magazines frequently rate guitar slingers, songs, bands, and albums as well as conduct readers' polls—both of which measure the impact of a performer on the heavy metal scene. The results of these surveys are like currency for performers. Young musicians in new bands benefit from the exposure, while readers learn to appreciate the historical significance of metal legends. Dime made regular appearances at the top of most magazine's guitar-related lists.

"... THE 1990S WILL BE KNOWN AS 'THE DECADE OF GREAT RIFFS BUT NO NEW LEAD GUITAR HEROES—EXCEPT ONE: DIMEBAG DARRELL ....'"

—NICK BOWCOTT, RIFFER MADNESS

Despite a brutal schedule on the road, Darrell took his column for *Guitar World* very seriously. He selected the topics several months in advance, then mulled each topic over with editor Nick Bowcott, who recorded Darrell's observations and points. Bowcott then transcribed these thoughts into column form and sent it to Dime, who made changes and corrections. Each column was full of strong advice for the serious player as well as a smattering of Dimebonics for color and humor.

THE LEGEND OF THE RAZORBACK

Darrell designed the Razorback at his home in Arlington in late 2004. After Rita worked out the negotiations with Dean Guitars, Dime drew the pattern life size on a sheet of paper, with Rita participating on the design for the headstock. When Dime was satisfied with the sketch, he cut out the life-size version on foam board and sent it to Dean. Zelinsky built the prototype by hand and sent it unfinished to Dime. Darrell held the prototype and let Zelinsky know he loved the guitar before returning it. Unfortunately, Darrell never had a chance to see the Razorback completely finished.

Bullseye

The **FIRST RAZORBACK** was given to Darrell's good friend **ZAKK WYLDE** of Black Label Society. Darrell had one **SPECIALLY MADE** for Wylde with a **BULLSEYE** design reminiscent of the Grail, the Les Paul guitar Zakk played while with Ozzy Osbourne's band. Sadly, Dime did not live to give it to his friend in person, but Dean Zelinsky and others made sure that Zakk received it. It was **PRESENTED TO HIM** on January 22, 2005, at the Dean booth at NAMM 2005. Rock photographer Chad Lee, a close personal friend of both Dime and Zakk, was there to capture the occasion.

The headstock of this specially made Bullseye Razorback reads, "**CUSTOM BUILT 4 ZAKK WYLDE AT THE REQUEST OF DIMEBAG.**"

RENAISSANCE
New Found Freedom

LEFT: IN 2003, DAMAGEPLAN WAS BORN. RIGHT: AT THE VERIZON WIRELESS THEATER IN HOUSTON ON APRIL 20, 2004, DAMAGEPLAN WAS FEATURED ON THE BILL WITH HATEBREED.

CHAPTER 8

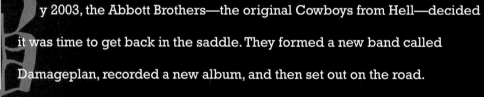

y 2003, the Abbott Brothers—the original Cowboys from Hell—decided it was time to get back in the saddle. They formed a new band called Damageplan, recorded a new album, and then set out on the road.

During the previous two years, frontman Phil Anselmo had immersed himself in several projects unrelated to Pantera. At first, he told the press that he considered Pantera his priority and that he had every intention of returning. In retrospect, it's clear that was not the case. He distanced himself from Pantera during interviews, declaring that the band had ac-

complished everything he could have hoped for, and that he was busy with other projects. Not wanting to disappoint the fans, or to give up their life's work, the Abbott Brothers repeatedly tried to reach out to Anselmo but to no avail. By 2002, Pantera was dissolved.

Darrell and Vinnie were naturally disheartened, having always assumed that Pantera would go on forever. Darrell told *Guitar World* magazine, "We honestly thought we were going to be the Rolling Stones of heavy metal." At ages 38 and 36, Vinnie and Darrell found it a challenge to start over—to muster the faith, strength and energy it would take to build a new band from the ground up. Dime in particular was reluctant to identify himself with any band but Pantera. However, Jerry Cantrell of Alice in Chains strongly advised them to move on—to create a new outlet for their energies and talents. With a nod to the future, Darrell and Vinnie formed Damageplan—a name that suggested to the world that the pair was planning to "destroy musically."

Two very distinctive musicians joined the Abbott Brothers' new venture. Bob Zilla was a long-

THE DYNAMIC BETWEEN BASSIST BOB ZILLA AND DARRELL IS OBVIOUS IN THIS CANDID SHOT OF THE PAIR ON STAGE. IN A 2007 INTERVIEW, ZILLA REMARKED, "HE WAS THE KIND OF PERSON THAT I STRIVED TO BE."

time friend who had been in several bands in the Dallas-Fort Worth area. Born Bob Kakaha, Zilla was also a tattoo artist who had done several of Dime's tattoos. The pair had grown quite close, and when Bob joined the band, Dime set him up in a house just three blocks away so he could be close by. Patrick Lachman had been the guitarist for the band Diesel Machine and then joined Halford, the self-named solo band of Judas Priest's vocalist Rob Halford. Just as word got out that Darrell and Vinnie were putting together a new group, Rob Halford announced that he was returning to Judas Priest, meaning Lachman was out of a gig. Though primarily known as a guitarist, Lachman had a thunderous voice and convinced Darrell and Vinnie that he could belt out tunes with a force and conviction that represented what the boys had always stood for—maximum heavy metal. He began sending tapes to Texas, and the Abbotts in turn sent him some songs to demo.

GUITARIST PAT LACHMAN HAD DONE VOCALS WHILE PERFORMING IN A PREVIOUS BAND, DIESEL MACHINE. HE LOBBIED HARD FOR THE JOB AS DAMAGEPLAN'S FRONTMAN, AND AFTER HE NAILED SEVERAL DEMOS WITH HIS POWERFUL VOICE, HE WAS HIRED.

Eventually, Lachman landed the coveted spot as the frontman for Damageplan.

From the beginning, Vinnie knew that Damageplan would not have the same chemistry and identity as Pantera. He and Darrell consciously attempted to develop a different style, and in doing so, they realized that starting over could be a liberating experience. Vinnie noted in an interview that Pantera had become limited, almost suffocating, because of its reputation for playing raw, abrasive metal. With Damageplan, he intended to expand the sound and style of Pantera so that the music was more challenging and more diverse. The pair were excited to get back to music with more melody and depth. As Dime revealed to *The Daily Advertiser*, "I went into this with a different mindset. I wanted to power-pack the leads between more hooky, catchy rhythms to reach as many people as we could."

In February 2004, Damageplan released *New Found Power*, their debut album on the Elektra label. From the titles of the songs to the sound of the music to the photo on the cover, the album fairly shouted that this was a new beginning for the Abbott Brothers. The cover image of Dime, Vinnie, Bob Zilla, and

Pat Lachman walking toward the viewer as they emerge from the billowing smoke left by an explosion suggested that the past had been destroyed, and the band was moving forward toward something new. Song titles such as "Breathing New Life," "New Found Power," and "Reborn" expressed an even stronger statement about starting over. Reviewers noticed the new musical direction and deemed several tunes, including "Moment of Truth" and "Save Me," more commercial than Pantera's last few albums, while still acknowledging Damageplan's metal roots. Many pointed to the poignant, haunting ballad "Soul Bleed," on which Dime plays acoustic guitar, as evidence of musical growth and depth for the Abbott Brothers.

Dime and Vinnie's friends and peers in the metal community were very supportive of their new band and their new direction, with several making guest appearances on the album. Zakk Wylde accompanied Damageplan on "Reborn" and "Soul Bleed," Corey Taylor of Slipknot sang on the confrontational anthem "Fuck You," and Jerry Cantrell of Alice in Chains helped out on "Ashes."

> "RISING FROM THE ASHES OF PANTERA, GUITARIST DIMEBAG DARRELL AND DRUMMER VINNIE PAUL HAVE RECONCILED HOOKINESS AND AGGRESSION ON THE DEBUT ALBUM FROM DAMAGEPLAN."
>
> —BILLBOARD, FEBRUARY 21, 2004

This time around, radio seemed more supportive of the music. "Save Me" in particular received considerable rock-radio airplay. The band had done a promotional tour, hitting radio stations for interviews in January, which boosted their recognition for the radio audience. They had also released a music

ON THE FIRST LEG OF THEIR FIRST TOUR AS DAMAGEPLAN, VINNIE, ZILLA, PAT LACHMAN, AND DIME CHECK OUT A NOODLE BAR IN JAPAN IN FEBRUARY 2004.

video for the song "Breathing New Life" for MTV's Headbangers' Ball. However, Vinnie and Darrell's approach to their new band and their loyal fans was to bring it to them live. They had always connected to their fan base through extensive touring, and they sought to maintain that direct relationship. On the heels of their debut album, Damageplan embarked on a worldwide tour, beginning in Japan and then joining MTV2's Headbangers' Ball Tour in the States. Darrell and Vinnie found themselves on the road with younger bands such as Hatebreed, Unearth, Drowning Pool, Shadows Fall, and The Haunted and the younger musicians invigorated them.

With Damageplan, Darrell and Vinnie returned to playing theaters and small arenas, which gave them a chance to get closer to the audiences. Of course, the fans still wanted to hear such classics as "Walk," "Cemetery Gates," and "Fucking Hostile," and Damageplan obliged. But the Abbotts understood it would take time and a full commitment of their hearts and souls before the fans could embrace Damageplan as they had Pantera.

Still, there was no major backlash from the fans. When audiences sang along with the band, Darrell and Vinnie noted that they could sing the words to Damageplan's songs just as well as they could shout out Pantera lyrics. More importantly, the fans realized that the music of Darrell and Vinnie was as exciting, creative, and powerful as ever. The Abbott Brothers were back, and the audiences loved it.

RELEASED FEBRUARY 10, 2004,
NEW FOUND POWER REACHED
THE TOP 40 ON THE BILLBOARD
200 ALBUMS CHART.

AS DAMAGEPLAN, PAT LACHMAN, VINNIE PAUL, BOB ZILLA, AND DIME WERE DETERMINED
TO CREATE AN IDENTITY THAT DIFFERED FROM THEIR PREVIOUS BANDS. IN A 2007 INTERVIEW,
VINNIE DECLARED THAT THIS BAND OFFERED HIM AND DIME THE OPPORTUNITY TO RETURN TO
THE MUSICIANSHIP THAT HAD ALWAYS BEEN AT THE ROOT OF THEIR MUSIC.

On tour for much of 2004, Damageplan played mostly their own tunes, with an occasional classic song such as "Walk" thrown in. The Damageplan song list can be seen taped to the amp on the left in this candid shot of the band on stage.

İn Dime's Words

"We Had to Move Forward"

With Damageplan on tour in Tokyo in 2004, Dime took time out to shoot a video on guitar techniques. In between lessons, he jokes with the crew and offers encouragement to the young guitar slingers who will be watching. He's as much at ease on camera as he is wailing on his axe, and as he walks through complex instructions on harmonics and echo techniques, he makes you feel like you're hanging out with some cool friend of your older brother. During one segment, he takes a few minutes to talk about Damageplan's first album in typical Dime fashion.

"I'm **DIMEBAG**. My new fuckin' band [is] **DAMAGEPLAN**. [Our] bad fuckin'-ass CD . . . is a very diverse record, not just one flavor. It's the full spectrum of rock—from all the way to hard-core to all the way to low-key, heartfelt shit . . . . '**NEW-FOUND POWER**' is the place that we had to come from once we hit the dirt and found out that it was the **END OF PANTERA**, and we had to **MOVE FORWARD**. It was the place inside our souls that we **HAD TO DIG DEEP**—new found power. [And] some of the greatest drummin' that I ever heard my brother do is on the [title] track."

145

BAND OF BROTHERS

From the beginning, Vinnie and Dime were the heart and soul of Pantera, just as they would be the backbone of Damageplan. As Vinnie would later recall, "We had an undeniable chemistry."

Left and bottom: While performing on stage, Dime would often turn to face Vinnie, and the two would play in a groove together that was a profound statement of their eternal bond as brothers.

As colleagues, friends, and brothers, Darrell and Vinnie were inseparable.

"[DARRELL'S] GUITAR LICKS WERE FLAWLESSLY CRUSHINGLY LINKED TO THE FURIOUS DRUMMING OF HIS BROTHER, VINNIE PAUL."

— MARK HOLMBERG, RICHMOND TIMES DISPATCH, DECEMBER 10, 2004

MIDDLE AND LEFT: BY THE TIME VINNIE AND DIME FORMED DAMAGEPLAN, THEY HAD BEEN MAKING MUSIC TOGETHER FOR OVER 20 YEARS. THEY WERE IN SYNC ONSTAGE AND OFF.

A Meeting of the Minds

During the course of their career, Darrell and Vinnie had met and worked with several of their idols—from Black Sabbath to Judas Priest to KISS. However, one major influence eluded them. They had never met Eddie and Alex VanHalen.

In late fall 2004, when Van Halen was playing Dallas, Eddie stopped by The Clubhouse and met Vinnie, but unfortunately Dime was in Arizona on business. Eddie invited the Abbotts to one of his upcoming Texas concerts, and the following week in Lubbock, the Van Halens and the Abbotts finally hooked up. By all reports, the two sets of brothers hit it off immediately, with Eddie exclaiming, "It's like we've known each other all our lives." The two guitar legends swapped licks and riffs, while all acknowledged the similarities between Eddie and Alex and Dime and Vinnie. After it was over, Dime confessed to Vinnie, "If a plane we were on crashed tomorrow, I'd die a happy man because I got to meet the guy who made me want to play the guitar."

DIME SMOKES ON ONE OF ED'S FRANKENSTRATS.

DIME, ALEX VAN HALEN, AND VINNIE (ABOVE) AND DIME, EDDIE VAN HALEN, AND VINNIE (RIGHT). THE TWO SETS OF BROTHERS HUNG OUT BACKSTAGE FOR SEVERAL HOURS BEFORE VAN HALEN'S BIG CONCERT IN LUBBOCK, TEXAS.

From a personal perspective, Dime was fulfilling a life-long dream when he finally met Eddie Van Halen. In a larger framework, it represented a truly historic moment. Eddie, a legend from an earlier generation of rock music, was literally meeting his legacy in Dime, a legend from a later generation influenced by him. On some level, both Dime and Eddie must have understood the symbolism of the moment for it represented how popular music evolves and expands by acknowledging and appreciating what came before.

Dime marks the occasion by having his picture taken in front of the set list for Van Halen's show that night in Lubbock.

BEHIND THE SCENES

DIME GAVE EVERYONE HE WORKED WITH A NICKNAME, WHICH WAS AKIN TO A BADGE OF HONOR. IT NOT ONLY REVEALED HIS QUICK WIT BUT ALSO HIS NATURAL FRIENDLINESS AND DESIRE TO BOND WITH PEOPLE HE CARED ABOUT.

BACKSTAGE AT THE 2004 SUMMERFEST, DIME ENJOYS A LAUGH WITH BOBBY TONGS, A CREW MEMBER SINCE THE EARLY DAYS WHO HELPED SHOOT MATERIAL FOR SOME OF THE BAND'S LEGENDARY VIDEOS.

GUY SYKES (LEFT) WORKED AS PANTERA'S TOUR MANAGER FOR MANY YEARS IN ADDITION TO SERVING AS A BASS GUITAR TECHNICIAN.

THE LOYAL CREW
Nicknames courtesy of Dime

GRADY CHAMPION
THE GRAND DRAGON: Guitar technician for Dime

JOHN BROOKS
JOHNNY KAT: Vinnie's long-time drum technician

GUY SYKES
SKY'S THE LIMIT: Tour manager

SONNY SATTERFIELD
LIGHTNING BRINGER or **GEORGE DICKLE:** Lighting tech

AARON BARNES
WIRES: Lighting tech and sound engineer

BRIAN JONES
BRIDOG: Roadie and confidant

DARRELL ARNBERGER
TONGS: Roadie and assistant to Dime on Dimevision videos

STERLING WINFIELD
C-RING: Recording engineer for Damageplan

VAL BIECHEKAS
BIG VAL: Security

WALT TRACHSLER
THE BROWN CLOWN: Roadie

GRADY CHAMPION WAS DIME'S GUITAR TECH FROM 1990 TO 2001.

FROM THE AGE OF 16, WALT TRACHSLER AND DIME WERE GOOD FRIENDS. WALT BECAME A ROADIE FOR PANTERA, EVENTUALLY WORKING HIS WAY UP TO OWNING HIS OWN BUS COMPANY. NOWADAYS, WALT OFTEN DRIVES THE BUS FOR VINNIE'S BAND, HELLYEAH.

Darrell heats up the Heartland one cool September night in Rockford, Illinois.

DIME OWNS THE STAGE AT
NUMBERS IN HOUSTON,
NOVEMBER 2, 2004.

DAMAGEPLAN

PAT LACHMAN (CALLED THE
LOCH NESS MONSTER BY DIME)
AND DIME ARE IN SYNC AT THE
HOUSE OF BLUES IN CHICAGO,
NOVEMBER 21, 2004.

AT THE END OF EACH SET, DAMAGEPLAN
PERFORMED THE METAL CLASSIC "WALK" FROM
1992'S *VULGAR DISPLAY OF POWER* ALBUM. AUDI-
ENCES WENT CRAZY AT THIS POINT IN THE SHOW,
BECAUSE "WALK" FEATURED ONE OF DIME'S MOST
FAMOUS RIFFS AND BECAUSE THE OTHER BANDS
ON THE BILL PLUS CREW MEMBERS AND FRIENDS
JOINED DAMAGEPLAN ON STAGE TO RENDER THIS
SIGNATURE TUNE.

REQUIEM
"We'll Meet Again"

CHAPTER 9

Every fan of Dimebag Darrell Abbott, Pantera, Damageplan, Gasoline, or heavy metal music knows what happened on December 8, 2004, at the nightclub Alrosa Villa in Worthington, Ohio, a working-class suburb of Columbus. The tragedy that resulted in Darrell's death occurred 24 years to the day after the murder of John Lennon and almost to the minute, an eerie coincidence that cast an even greater pall over the event.

In retrospect, the events of that one day have overshadowed the last year of Darrell's amazing career. Accounts of his life tend to jump from his

DIMEBAG DARRELL ABBOTT: GUITAR GENIUS, PARTY ANIMAL, METAL ICON, GENTLE SOUL . . .
GONE TOO SOON.

accomplishments with Pantera to his death, with only a nominal mention of Damageplan and the previous months of that year. Those who emphasize the terrible nature of the tragedy opt for a bitter conclusion that robs his story of the achievements and the triumph over adversity that Damageplan represents.

To start over with a new band after being affiliated with a world-renowned group for almost 20 years was challenging enough, but to endure the constant comparisons to the past and the unpredictable expectations of the fans made the task monumental. Not only did Darrell and Vinnie meet those challenges, they used the opportunity to reconnect with their musicianship and explore a new musical direction with Damageplan without turning their backs on heavy metal. It was a fine line to "Walk," as goes the title of one of their most memorable tunes.

Damageplan and the Abbott Brothers earned the respect of most reviewers, including those at *Billboard* magazine who recognized that Darrell and Vinnie had integrated the aggression of their earlier work with a new "hookiness." The result was a melodic sound with greater possibilities, including broader radio-play. During the early 1990s, the

Abbotts and Pantera had pushed heavy metal to its extreme at a time when many groups had abandoned it and it was in danger of extinction; in the early 2000s, when that direction had gone as far as it could, they steered metal in another direction that could have been equally influential if Damageplan had continued.

The support and respect that the Abbotts garnered among their peers is evident on *New Found Power*, in which metal stalwarts Zakk Wylde, of Ozzy Osbourne's band and later Black Label

Just a few months before the tragedy, Dime surprised Zakk Wylde backstage with framed portraits of legendary metal guitar slinger Randy Rhoads.

CHRISTENED "THE TRIPLE THREAT" BY DIME, THIS PHOTO TAKEN
BACKSTAGE AUGUST 8, 2004, CAPTURES THREE OF METAL'S GREAT-
EST SHREDDERS, DIME, ZAKK WYLDE, AND KERRY KING. ACCORD-
ING TO PHOTOGRAPHER CHAD LEE, IT WAS THE ONLY TIME THE
THREE WERE PHOTOGRAPHED TOGETHER—A ONCE-IN-A-LIFETIME
OPPORTUNITY.

Society, and Scott Ian of Anthrax made guest appearances. The formation of Damageplan not only
offered the Abbotts an opportunity to reflect on their
careers but also for the rest of the metal community
to assess the impact of the brothers from Texas on
their genre of music. From the biggest names in
metal like Wylde, Ian, and Kerry King of Slayer to
the younger metal bands such as Drowning Pool and
Shadows Fall, Darrell and Vinnie had the support
and respect of all. That was the state of affairs
throughout 2004 when Damageplan toured in support of *New Found Power.* It had been a year of
reflection, assessment, and reinvigoration—and this
is an important era of Darrell's career that should not
be overshadowed by previous accomplishments.

Damageplan toured heavily in 2004, including
the "Devastation Across the Nation" tour that had
begun in Madison, Wisconsin, on July 24. The band
had played in 45 cities, all one-night-stands. The gig
on December 8th at the Alrosa Villa, which had been
an add-on and not part of the original tour, was the
next-to-the-last date before the band was to return
home to Arlington, Texas, to enjoy the holidays.

What should have been just one more show
turned into a tragedy of epic proportions when a
mentally disturbed ex-Marine named Nathan Gale
fatally shot Darrell, along with Damageplan security
head Jeffery "Mayhem" Thompson, Alrosa security
man Erin Halk, and audience member Nathan Bray.
Two others, band manager Chris Paluska and drum
tech Johnny "Kat" Brooks, were seriously wounded.
Brooks was being held hostage by Gale when police
officer James Niggemeyer put an end to the ordeal
by fatally shooting the gunman.

Speculation about Gale's motive ran rampant
in the press and among fans for several months.
Reporters erroneously referred to Gale as an ob-
sessed Pantera fan who was angry over the break up
of the band, but the ex-Marine was actually a para-
noid schizophrenic who had been struggling with
his condition since childhood. According to Chris

Armold, who wrote the most detailed account of the tragedy to date in *A Vulgar Display of Power: Courage and Carnage at the Alrosa Villa*, Gale was discharged from the military because of his condition and had apparently stopped taking his medication. He was under the delusion that Pantera band members had been spying on him and had stolen his thoughts to compose the lyrics to their songs.

A great metal warrior had fallen, and outpourings of grief over the death of Dimebag Darrell

THE OTHER VICTIMS OF THE SHOOTING INCLUDED JOHNNY "KAT" BROOKS, SHOWN HERE SINGING "WALK" ON STAGE WITH DIME, AND JEFFERY "MAYHEM" THOMPSON, IN THE PHOTO AT RIGHT. THOMPSON, WHO WORKED SECURITY FOR DAMAGEPLAN, COURAGEOUSLY SACRIFICED HIS LIFE TO PROTECT OTHERS.

JUST A FEW DAYS BEFORE THE ALROSA VILLA GIG, EXCERPTS FROM AN INTERVIEW THAT PHIL ANSELMO GAVE TO *METAL HAMMER* MAGAZINE WERE RELEASED. BITTER AND ANGRY, PHIL HAD LET LOOSE WITH SEVERAL INCENDIARY COMMENTS, INCLUDING A STATEMENT THAT DARRELL SHOULD BE "SEVERELY BEATEN." AFTER THE TRAGEDY THOSE WORDS WOULD COME BACK TO HAUNT HIM FOR ETERNITY. ANSELMO WAS NOT WELCOME AT THE FUNERAL OR THE PUBLIC MEMORIAL.

Abbott poured in immediately from all over the metal community. Typical of the verbal tributes was an official statement by Lars Ulrich posted on Metallica's website, "Darrell and his brother were the cornerstone of musical adventures that were always groundbreaking, pushing boundaries, challenging to themselves and to their fans, respected by their peers and always true musicians' musicians." Metal musicians were shocked at the circumstances of his death, perhaps realizing it could have happened to any one of them. Mostly, they were saddened at the loss of an amazing guitar player, a true influence on the genre, and a gentle soul.

"YOU WERE THE PEOPLE'S ROCK STAR."

— MESSAGE LEFT BY A FAN ON DARRELL'S MAILBOX

On December 14, Dimebag Darrell was laid to rest in a private service at a funeral home in Arlington. Attendees included family, friends, band mates, and peers. The service was scheduled for 3:33 p.m., because three was Dime's favorite number, though in keeping with his habit of always being late, the proceedings did not start till after 4:00 p.m. It was a funeral befitting a rock star of Dime's caliber: He was buried in a KISS-themed casket in his camouflage pants and Black Label Society vest. Mourners filled the casket with bottles of Crown Royal, Judas Priest's *Metalogy* box set, and a guitar pedal. In a stunning tribute, Eddie Van Halen placed his Frankenstrat, his black-and-yellow striped guitar, in the casket, while Zakk Wylde, Anthrax drummer Charlie Benante, Alice in Chains guitarist Jerry Cantrell, Nick Bowcott, and Van Halen himself spoke to the grieving mourners. Cantrell, Alice in Chains bass player Mike Inez, Dime's friend Shawn Matthews, and Pat Lachman gave an accoustic performance of "Brother" and "Got Me Wrong." At the gravesite in Moore Memorial Gardens Cemetery, a tribute was read, and then each person was given a Black-Tooth Grin, which they downed in one gulp in Darrell's honor.

That evening, a public memorial was held at the Arlington Civic Arena, with about 5,000 fans in attendance. Blow-ups of guitar-magazine covers that showcased Dime were on display, and his famous Dean from Hell sat at the front of the stage. Again, Eddie Van Halen spoke, as did Zakk Wylde and Nick Bowcott, who had worked with Dime on his columns for *Guitar World*.

But the evening belonged to Vinnie Paul when he brought the house down by paying a simple tribute to his band mate, friend, and brother. After leading the crowd in a chant of "Dimebag," he noted, "The brightest star in Texas is shining tonight. That's my brother, Dimebag."

DARRELL WAS BURIED NEXT TO HIS MOTHER, NORMA CAROLYN ABBOTT, IN MOORE MEMORIAL GARDENS CEMETERY. SHORTLY AFTER THE INTERMENT, FANS PAID THEIR RESPECTS BY LEAVING TOKENS OF THEIR APPRECIATION AND AFFECTION, INCLUDING PHOTOS, MEMENTOES, — AND DIMES.

✝ Testament

The monumental outpouring of grief over Darrell's passing came from all corners of the globe. Some are a testament to the musician; others are a testament to the man.

"I'M ABSOLUTELY BESIDE MYSELF WITH GRIEF." —OZZY OSBOURNE

"[Dime and Vinnie] had a wonderful passion for their work and for the DALLAS STARS. They weren't just hockey fans, they were friends of the entire team. Dime will be missed very much." — **CRAIG LUDWIG**, *former member of the Dallas Stars*

"Darrell was a living legend . . . The world has lost a great human being."
— DEAN ZELINSKY, founder of DEAN GUITARS

"He wasn't just a player that all guitarists aspired to be, but the genuine article and a true friend." **—DROWNING POOL**

"On behalf of my family, my clan relations (Ta'neezahni nishlo), and the entire NAVAJO NATION, thanks for all the laughs, all the jamming, all the energy you gave us all, Dime. You will be sorely missed.
—Fan Erik Bitsui, Letter to the Editor of the *Farmington Daily Times*

"HARD ROCK HAS LOST A LEGENDARY PLAYER."
—TOM CALDERONE, MTV VICE-PRESIDENT

"... one of the most influential guitarists of his particular generation."
—Brad Tolinksi, GUITAR WORLD, Editor-in-Chief

"DIMEBAG" •
DARRELL LANCE ABBOTT

AUG. 20
1966

DEC. 8
2004

1966   2004

DIMEBAG DARRELL

HE CAME TO ROCK...
AND ROCKED LIKE NO OTHER...
WITH THE HEART TWICE THE
SIZE OF TEXAS, OUR BELOVED
BROTHER, COMPANION, MENTOR,
IDOL, AND FRIEND...
WE LOVE YOU DIME...
UNTIL WE MEET AGAIN

FANS STILL HONOR DIME BY LEAV-
ING TOKENS AT HIS GRAVE SITE,
WHICH OFTEN HAVE A SPECIFIC
CONNOTATION RELATED TO DIME'S
CAREER OR LARGER-THAN-LIFE
PERSONALITY. EVERYTHING FROM
GUITAR PICKS TO DIMES TO THE
MAKINGS FOR A BLACK-TOOTH
GRIN HAVE ADORNED HIS GRAVE.

Dimebag

August 20, 1966 – December 8, 2004

THE MEMORIAL NOTE FROM THE
SERVICE FEATURED THIS SHOT BY
ROCK PHOTOGRAPHER CHAD LEE.
THE PHOTO HAS SINCE TAKEN ON
A LIFE OF ITS OWN, BECOMING AN
ICONIC IMAGE OF DARRELL'S LOVE
OF LIFE AND MUSIC.

Darrell Lance Abbott

~ Born ~
August Twentieth
Nineteen Hundred Sixty-Six
Grand Prairie, Texas

~ Taken ~
December Eighth
Two Thousand Four
Columbus, Ohio

~ Services ~
3:33 pm
Tuesday, December Fourteenth
Moore Funeral Home Chapel

~ Interment ~
Moore Memorial Gardens
Arlington, Texas

"Always keep on keepin' on
no matter what—
keep on keepin' on."

On December 14, 2004, about 5,000 fans joined heavy metal royalty at the Arlington Convention Center to say good-bye to Dimebag Darrell Abbott. They ranged in age from young children to middle-aged adults. Some wore black rock t-shirts, while others were dressed in business suits; some waited in the cold for hours to get in, while others drove to Arlington from surrounding states. But they all shared in common a desire to pay their respects to someone whose music had been the soundtrack to their lives.

THREE HUGE SCREENS WITH PHOTOS OF DARRELL WERE MOUNTED BEHIND THE STAGE IN THE CENTER'S GRAND HALL. FLANKING THE STAGE WERE A NUMBER OF POSTER-SIZE MAGAZINE COVERS FEATURING DIME.

SIX VANS CARRIED OVER 100 FLOWER ARRANGEMENTS TO THE CENTER, INCLUDING THOSE WITH CROWN ROYAL MOTIFS AND GUITAR-SHAPED DISPLAYS.

WRITER NICK BOWCOTT BOWS
DOWN AND PAYS HOMAGE TO
DIME'S DEAN FROM HELL, WHICH
WAS PROMINENTLY DISPLAYED.

EDDIE VAN HALEN AND ZAKK WYLDE TRADED ANECDOTES
ABOUT DIME FOR THE CROWD. VAN HALEN HELD HIS CELL
PHONE TO THE MICROPHONE TO PLAY A MESSAGE THAT DIME
HAD LEFT HIM THE WEEK BEFORE HIS DEATH. THE CROWD
ROARED WHEN THEY HEARD HIS VOICE.

MIKE INEZ, JERRY
CANTRELL, PAT LACHMAN,
AND SHAWN MATTHEWS
PLAY AN ACOUSTIC SET TO
HONOR ONE OF THEIR OWN.

163

A Farewell from the Fans

After Darrell's death, avid fans left heartfelt messages, tributes, and messages at the gates to his home in Arlington.

Chris Armold, author of *A Vulgar Display of Power: Carnage and Courage at the Alrosa Villa*, left a signed copy of his book at the grave site as a tribute to Dime.

One of the most haunting tribute sites for Darrell is the back door of the Alrosa Villa, where heartbroken fans come from miles around to express their sorrow.

"Rest in peace, Dimebag Darrell. Your musical legacy lives on in the hearts—and ears—of your fans."
—Rina Omar, *New Straits Times Press* (Malaysia)

LEGACY
Infinite Shadow

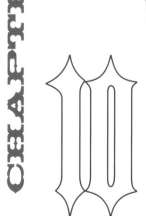
Texas has a long tradition of guitar slingers, especially those steeped in the soulful sounds of the blues. Ever since legendary bluesman Robert Johnson recorded 29 songs in Dallas and San Antonio in 1936–1937, a steady procession of guitar players have called the Lone Star State their home—from Albert Collins to Stevie Ray Vaughan to Johnny Winter to Bugs Henderson to Rocky Athas to Dimebag Darrell Abbott. Though their genres of music are different, they are all links in a vibrant musical culture and heritage. Dime not only absorbed the influences of those who came

DIME'S PEERS, FRIENDS, AND FAMILY REMEMBER HIS KIND-HEARTED, GENEROUS PERSONALITY, WHICH WAS PART OF THE REASON HE MADE SUCH A LASTING INFLUENCE ON THE HEAVY-METAL COMMUNITY. BUT HIS TRUE LEGACY IS THE MUSIC.

before him but he passed on his own to new generations of guitar players.

Dime's legacy is the music—not only his specific riffs and solos but the undertones of his style that reflect regional sounds and genres, such as the blues or Texas-style rock 'n' roll. These contributions elevated the artistry of heavy metal, a genre of music often slighted by the music industry and snubbed by the mainstream press. That was his gift to heavy metal specifically and to popular music in general.

It was a gift recognized by the Texas Music Office under Governor Rick Perry, which named Darrell Lance Abbott a "Texas Music Pioneer." According to the Music Office, a Pioneer is a Texan who has "made significant contributions to the art or business of music." As declared by the Music Office, "Abbott's heavy but melodic style led to his being recognized as one of the top ten metal guitarists of all time by *Guitar Player* magazine."

Dime's talents and musicianship were not the only ways that he proved influential. He and Vinnie gained a reputation for serving as mentors to Texas-based bands such as Pumpjack and Drowning Pool,

IN THE MONTHS AFTER HIS DEATH, ALL THE MAJOR GUITAR MAGA-ZINES WERE QUICK TO ASSESS THE CAREER, MUSICIANSHIP, AND INFLUENCE OF DIMEBAG DARRELL ABBOTT.

guiding them in the ways and wiles of the music industry. They used their pull to persuade record execs to come to Texas to check out the local talent. Linda Hollar, publisher of the Dallas-based magazine *Harder Beat,* remarked to the *Dallas Morning News* in 1997, "[The Abbotts] are very visible. They're out in the clubs; everybody knows them. They're the hometown boys who made good. That's why they're such an influence to all the bands."

Drowning Pool became especially successful,

going on to sell millions of records, while Pumpjack was hired by Darrell and Vinnie as the opening act for Pantera in the late 1990s. The Abbotts were also able to get Pumpjack into Ozzfest one year. As an ever-lasting show of support, Dime worked Pumpjack into the lyrics of the song "N.Y.C. Streets," a song he recorded with David Allan Coe that was later released on the *Rebel Meets Rebel* album.

Often Dime's support of Texas-based musicians came in the form of jamming with them at clubs and bars. He was fond of dropping by the metal clubs when he was in town just to sit in on a song or two. His impromptu jam sessions with locals go back to the 1980s and the notorious club known as The Basement, but long after his success, he never ceased to play along with up-and-coming bands. He was motivated by his own experiences, having had the support of his father Jerry to help his career and the encouragement of local musicians such as Ricky Lynn Gregg to inspire him. Dime was the perfect role model because he was driven to succeed, remained passionate about his music, and was determined to be a true friend to all local musicians.

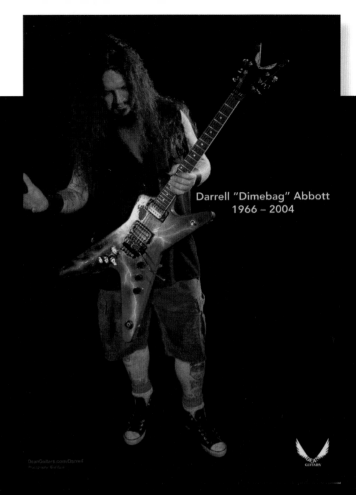

Darrell "Dimebag" Abbott
1966 – 2004

DeanGuitars.com/Darrell

DEAN ZELINSKY ISSUED THIS EFFECTIVE TRIBUTE TO DIME IN THE NAME OF DEAN GUITARS. THE PHOTO OF DARRELL LOST IN REVERIE AS HE PLAYS HIS DEAN FROM HELL MAKES FOR A TIMELESS IMAGE OF A ROCK LEGEND, WHILE THE SIMPLE TEXT SERVES AS A MEMORIAL AND A REMINDER THAT HE WAS TAKEN FAR TOO SOON.

Outside the borders of Texas, Dime's metal musicianship and humanity are still recognized around the world by the guitar superstars who are the backbone of big-name bands, including Michael Schenker of the Scorpions, Dave Mustaine of Megadeth, Lars Ulrich of Metallica, and Yngwie J. Malmsteen. The names that appeared over and over on Dime's list of personal favorites became the same

BOB ZILLA ON HIS FRIEND AND BAND MATE: "[DIME] HAD THE MAGIC... HE WAS A GUY WHO COULD MAKE ANYBODY FEEL LIKE HIS BEST FRIEND IN THREE MINUTES."

players who accurately and astutely articulated his contributions to metal after his death. The respect and admiration of these legendary musicians for Dime was revealed in the 6-String Masterpiece Collection, an exhibit of guitars custom-painted by rock guitarists in Darrell's honor that toured the world in 2005 and 2006.

So it was that local musicians appreciated Dimebag Darrell Abbott's generosity and ability to serve as a role model while internationally renowned guitarists understood his talents and contributions to metal. But in the months and years after his death,

perhaps the most poignant statements about Dime came from the musicians who knew him personally. Not always as expressive as those who are accustomed to making statements before the press and public, they made up for it with a direct sincerity that perfectly conveys Dime's true nature and unique gifts.

In an exclusive interview in 2007, Bob Zilla talked about Dimebag Darrell, his friend and fellow band member. Currently the bass player for Hellyeah, Zilla had known the Abbotts for many years and had a front-row seat to their ups and downs. As a member of Damageplan, he was there the night of the tragedy when Dime lost his life at the Alrosa Villa. Zilla confesses that he was mostly in awe of Darrell's generosity as a human being and his capacity to respond to fans. He witnessed many times when Dime was so exhausted he could barely move, but he would pause and take photos with fans or sign as many t-shirts as they would put in front of him. "He showed me the person that I should strive to be," said Zilla. "He was the perfect example of the guy that had everything—and could have anything—and all he cared about were his friends and his music and trying to bridge them together."

When asked to describe Dime's impact on heavy metal, Zilla found a unique way to summarize the enormity of that influence with a simple declaration of awe and sentiment. "I don't think I should answer that question," said Zilla, "because it's out there right now as we're sitting here . . . . Just listen to music now; it speaks for itself . . . I don't have to say anything because it is being said in the music. All the albums and songs and bands that are out there now are answering that question as we speak."

VINNIE PAUL AND JERRY (AKA L.D.) PROUDLY SHOW OFF ONE OF DARRELL'S GUITARS, WHICH IS ON DISPLAY IN ITS RIGHTFUL HOME, THE ROCK 'N' ROLL HALL OF FAME IN CLEVELAND, OHIO.

Scott Ian of Anthrax: "[As a musician, Dime] had everything—just his originality, the riffs he wrote, his tone, and what he did with his guitar. He didn't sound like anybody before him, and nobody could come close to duplicating what he did. That's the best thing you could say about any musician . . . ." (*Rolling Stone* website)

Zakk Wylde of Black Label Society: ". . . [Dime's] right up there with Eddie and Randy and Hendrix . . . [and] he was a ray of sunshine . . . ." (*Rolling Stone* website)

"He's just a genuinely good guy and great musician."

—Ace Frehley (at Dime's Rock Walk Induction)

"Darrell and his brother (drummer Vinnie Paul Abbott) were the cornerstone of musical adventures that were always groundbreaking, pushing boundaries, challenging to themselves and to their fans, respected by their peers and always true musicians' musicians."

—Lars Ulrich, Metallica, *San Francisco Chronicle*

"Dime's music was a huge influence on me personally and on Lamb of God as a whole. As a guitar player, he was a true innovator. His sound, tone, and style shaped modern metal . . . ."

—Mark Morton, Lamb of God (www.dimebageternal.com)

"[Dime] changed the way metal music was written with his guitar playing. I don't know anybody in a band who hasn't stolen a few guitar riffs from him."

—Mark Hunter, Chimaira (Associated Press)

". . . I proudly say that he's one of the most skilled and technically proficient guitar players I have ever seen."

—Yngwie J. Malmsteen (www.damageplan.com)

GUITARISTS OF OUR DAY. HE WAS JUST A LEGEND."

—JONATHAN DAVIS, KORN (*ROLLING STONE* WEBSITE)

On February 23, 2005, a benefit concert was held at Chicago's Aragon Ballroom.
David Draiman of Disturbed organized the benefit, gathering together some of
Dime's friends and peers to play in his honor.

Disturbed, Anthrax, Soil, and Drowning Pool were in the line-up at the Aragon. Backstage, some of the band members and crew marked the occasion with Rita (second from
left) and Vinnie (holding sign). That night Vinnie, Pat Lachman, and Bob Zilla sat in with
Anthrax on "A New Level" and with Disturbed on "Walk," which was the first time any of
them had performed since the tragedy.

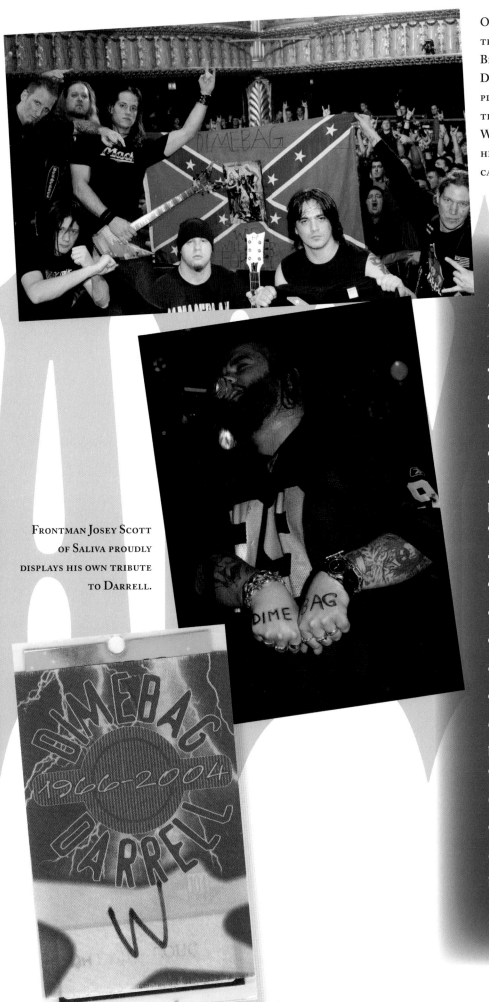

ON DECEMBER 10, 2004—TWO DAYS AFTER THE TRAGEDY—A SHOW AT THE CHICAGO HOUSE OF BLUES TURNED INTO AN EMOTIONAL TRIBUTE TO DIME. DAMAGEPLAN HAD BEEN SCHEDULED TO PLAY, BUT IN THE AFTERMATH OF THE TRAGEDY, THE OTHER ARTISTS INCLUDING SOIL, KENNY WAYNE SHEPPARD, AND SALIVA, CONTINUED ON IN HIS SPIRIT. A FAN MADE THE BANNER, WHICH WAS CARRIED ONSTAGE DURING SOIL'S SET.

FRONTMAN JOSEY SCOTT OF SALIVA PROUDLY DISPLAYS HIS OWN TRIBUTE TO DARRELL.

TRIBUTE SONGS
to Dimebag Darrell Abbott

"IN THIS RIVER" by Zakk Wylde
on Black Label Society's album *Mafia*

"DEIFY" by Disturbed
on *Ten Thousand Fists*

"DIMEBAG"
by Cross Canadian Ragweed
on *Garage*

"SIDE OF A BULLET" by Nickelback
on *All the Right Reasons*

"TO THE FALLEN HERO" by God Forbid
on *IV: Constitution of Treason*

"BETRAYED" by Avenged Sevenfold
on *City of Evil*

"DIME'S IN HEAVEN"
by Brides of Destruction
on *Runaway Brides*

"BEHIND THE STONE" by M.S.
on *A Breath of Fresh Air*

"LETTER TO DIMEBAG"
by Brian Welch, formerly of Korn

REBEL MEETS REBEL

Around the year 2000, Darrell and country-music renegade David Allan Coe began composing and recording songs together at Dime's studio. In 2006, Vinnie released 12 of the songs on an album called *Rebel Meets Rebel*. Coe and Dime were kindred spirits whose musical talents and instincts clicked. The old country outlaw's inclinations toward pushing the boundaries of country music made him open to Dime's metal style, while working with Coe afforded Darrell the opportunity to reach beyond metal riffs and solos.

Dime met David Allan Coe when he and Vinnie went to see the country outlaw at Billy Bob's Texas in Fort Worth. Dime loved the show and afterward waited in line like everyone else to get an autograph and to give DAC some Pantera CDs. The two hit it off immediately. Later that night, DAC popped in the Pantera CD, and it floored him. He later told Dime and Vinnie, "It was like not knowing who the Beatles were and just discovering them." The next day, he called Dime, and the two decided to write some songs together ... *Rebel Meets Rebel* was born!!!!

"[REBEL MEETS REBEL] HAS GOT SOME OF DIME'S BEST GUITAR WORK...."

—VINNIE PAUL, DALLAS MORNING NEWS, APRIL 24, 2006

VINNIE RELEASED *REBEL MEETS REBEL* ON HIS OWN LABEL, BIG VIN RECORDS. AS VINNIE DESCRIBED THE ALBUM TO *BILLBOARD*, "SOME OF THE SONGS ARE ABOUT GAMBLING, SOME OF THEM ARE ABOUT BROKEN HEARTS AND SOME ARE ABOUT DRINKING. THERE'S STUFF ON THERE THAT'S BALLS-OUT METAL, AND THERE'S STUFF THAT'S COUNTRY. THERE'S EVEN A FLAMENCO GUITAR SONG."

MISS KIM AND DR. ROCK, THE DEEJAY AT THE CLUBHOUSE, HAVE STARS IN THEIR EYES STANDING NEXT TO DAVID ALLAN COE AND VINNIE PAUL. COE WROTE A SPECIAL MESSAGE TO DIME IN THE LINER NOTES OF *REBEL MEETS REBEL*: "IN MEMORY OF DIMEBAG—I LOVE YOU."

THE RELEASE PARTY WAS HELD AMID A HIGHLY FESTIVE ATMOSPHERE AT THE CLUBHOUSE IN DALLAS. COE IS ACCOMPANIED BY HIS PARTNER IN CRIME MISS KIM, WHILE VINNIE AND VIDEO BOB OF BIG VIN RECORDS ENSURE THAT EVERYONE HAD A GOOD TIME.

Six-String Masterpieces

In 2006, Dean Guitars and the creative director of the Action Arts Agency, Chris "Curse" Mackey, collaborated on a unique tribute to Dimebag Darrell Abbott—an exhibit of Dean ML guitars, each painted by a different rock star or tattoo artist. Everyone from Rob Zombie to Kelly Clarkson participated by painting or creating a guitar. The exhibit toured around the country as part of Ozzfest 2006, the Family Values Tour, South by Southwest, the Dallas International Guitar Festival, MusikMesse (Frankfurt, Germany), the London Guitar Show, the Rock Festival in Tokyo, and the Headbangers' Ball tour. "Six-String Masterpieces" was arguably the most viewed art exhibit of 2006.

THE GUITARS WERE AUCTIONED OFF IN MAY 2007, WITH PROCEEDS GOING TO THE LITTLE KIDS ROCK FOUNDATION, A CHARITY FOUNDED BY DAVID WISH THAT PROVIDES FREE INSTRUMENTS AND MUSIC LESSONS TO CHILDREN IN UNDERSERVED PUBLIC SCHOOLS. THE AUCTION RAISED ENOUGH MONEY TO OPEN CHAPTERS OF LITTLE KIDS ROCK—IN TAMPA, FLORIDA, AND IN DALLAS.

SOME OF THE TREATMENTS THAT THE ROCK STARS AND TATTOO ARTISTS CAME UP WITH WERE ELEGANTLY SIMPLE, AS WITH BILLY CORGAN'S DESIGN FEATURING WHITE CROSSES ON A BLACK BACKGROUND, WHILE OTHERS WERE MORE COLORFUL OR COMPLEX, SUCH AS TATTOO ARTIST JACK RUDY'S RENDERING OF A SKULL-LIKE FACE WITH FLAMES (FAR RIGHT).

Participating Artists

AARON CAIN (Aaron Cain Tattoo), ALEXI LAIHO (Children of Bodom), BILLY CORGAN (Smashing Pumpkins), BOB TYRRELL, BOB ZILLA (Damageplan), CHARLIE BENANTE (Anthrax), CHEST BENNINGTON (Linkin Park), DAN DONEGAN (Disturbed), DAVE GROHL (Foo Fighters), DAVE NAVARRO (Jane's Addiction), DAVID STOUPAKIS (Deftones), DEREK HESS (Derek Hess Studios), FILIP LEU (Leu Family Iron), GILL MONTIE, GREG TRIBBETT (Mudvayne), GUY AITCHISON (Hyperspace Studios), HANK WILLIAMS III, JACK RUDY, JAMES HETFIELD (Metallica), JASON D'AQUINO (Blue Moon Tattoo), JERRY CANTRELL (Alice in Chains), JIM ROOT (Slipknot), JOE CAPOBIANCO (Hope Gallery), JOE SATRIANI, JONATHAN DAVIS (Korn), KELLY CLARKSON, KERRY KING (Slayer), KIRK HAMMETT (Metallica), MARILYN MANSON, MARK MOTHERSBAUGH (Devo), MICHAEL ANTHONY (Van Halen), MICK THOMPSON (Slipknot), JOE HAHN (Linkin Park), MOBY, JAMES "MUNKY" SHAFFER (Korn), ODERUS URUNGUS (Gwar), OTEP, PAUL BOOTH (Last Rites Tattoo), ROB ZOMBIE, RON ENGLISH (Popaganda Art Studio), RYAN MCGINNESS, SAMMY HAGAR, SAS CHRISTIAN (Hotbox Designs), SHANNON LARKIN (Godsmack), SHAWN CRAHAN (Slipknot), STEVE STEVENS (Billy Idol Band), SULLY ERNA (Godsmack), SUM 41, TED NUGENT, TOM MORELLO (Audioslave), WILLIE ADLER (Lamb of God), and ZAKK WYLDE (Black Label Society)

TOP LEFT: DESIGN BY FORMER VAN HALEN FRONT MAN SAMMY HAGAR. TOP RIGHT: DESIGN BY ROCK LEGEND TED NUGENT.
BOTTOM LEFT: DESIGN BY BOB TYRRELL. BOTTOM RIGHT: DESIGN BY ZAKK WYLDE OF BLACK LABEL SOCIETY.

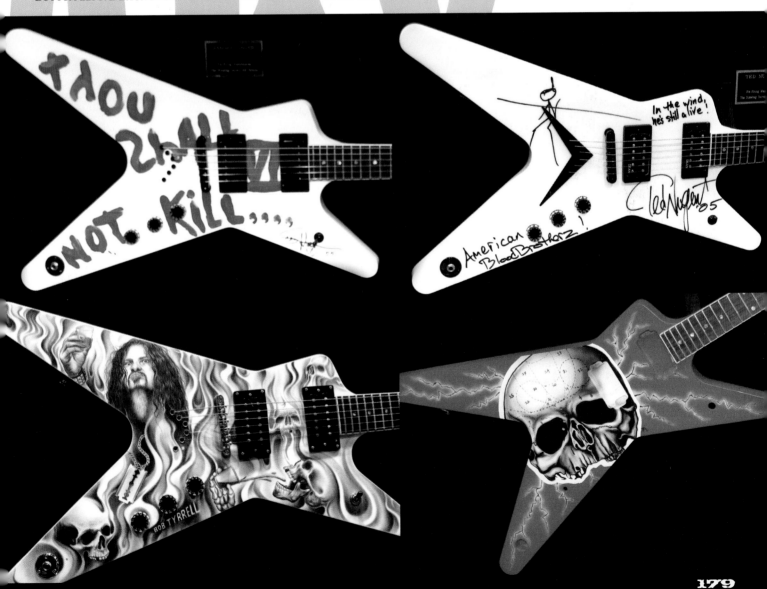

On May 17, 2007, Dimebag Darrell Abbott was inducted into Hollywood's RockWalk, a sidewalk gallery dedicated to the giants of rock music. Organized by the Guitar Center in Hollywood, RockWalk became a reality in November 1985 with the inaugural inductions of Eddie Van Halen, Stevie Wonder, and Gibson Les Paul guitar creator Ted McCarty, among others. RockWalk's nominees are selected by those previously inducted, which means inductees are chosen by musicians and musical authorities.

VINNIE, RITA, AND JERRY DISPLAY A FRAMED DECLARATION OF DIME'S INAUGURATION INTO THE ROCKWALK.

MANY OF HEAVY METAL'S LEADING MUSICIANS ATTENDED THE FESTIVITIES. BACK ROW, FROM LEFT: ACE FREHLEY OF KISS, JOHN 5, JERRY CANTRELL OF ALICE IN CHAINS, ZAKK WYLDE, AND ROCK WRITER NICK BOWCOTT. MIDDLE: VINNIE, JERRY, RITA, AND AARON LEWIS FROM STAIND. FRONT: SCOTT IAN OF ANTHRAX, MIKE INEZ OF ALICE IN CHAINS, AND KERRY KING OF SLAYER.

During the ceremony, Zakk Wylde offered a moving performance of "In This River," a song that became associated with Dime after his death. According to Wylde, the song will never leave the play list for Black Label Society.

One legend speaks on another: Darrell's childhood hero Ace Frehley not only attended the ceremony but spoke a few words in tribute to Dime.

Among those who attended the ceremony were Kerry King and Dean Zelinsky of Dean Guitars—both notables from the music industry and good friends to Dime.

181

THE MANY FACES OF DIME

Over the years, several professional rock photographers got their opportunity to capture Dimebag Darrell, wielding his axe. Though the subject was the same, each photographer zeroed in on something different about Dime, whether it was his charisma, his sense of humor, his humanity, or his musical genius.

TEXAN AND NOTED ROCK PHOTOGRAPHER STUART TAYLOR KNEW DARRELL BACK IN THE DAY OF POODLE PERMS AND SPANDEX PANTS. TAYLOR RECALLS, "HE WEAVED HIS MAGIC INTO MANY LIVES AND I WAS ONE OF THE LUCKY PEOPLE WHO GOT TO SPEND A GREAT PART OF MY LIFE WITH A GREAT GUY. THERE IS NOT A DAY THAT GOES BY THAT I DO NOT THINK ABOUT THE PERSON WHO WAS THE SINGLE MOST POSITIVE INFLUENCE IN MY LIFE . . . ."

THROUGH ZAKK WYLDE, CHAD LEE BECAME FRIENDS WITH DARRELL DURING THE DAMAGEPLAN ERA. THOUGH LEE TOOK HUNDREDS OF SHOTS OF DIMEBAG THE GUITAR GOD, HIS PERSONAL RELATIONSHIP ALLOWED HIM TO CAPTURE DIME'S SENSE OF HUMOR. CHAD SNAPPED DIME IN ARLINGTON AT ELKINS PARK LAKE ON OCTOBER 23, 2004—SHORTLY BEFORE DIME CHASED THOSE UNSUSPECTING DUCKS INTO THE LAKE.

MATTHEW SALACUSE'S PORTRAITS ARE SPECIFICALLY COMPOSED AND DRAMATICALLY LIT IN ORDER TO CAPTURE THE PERSONA OF A HEAVY METAL GIANT.

MAURO ALVAREZ PHOTOGRAPHED DARRELL ONLY DURING THE DAMAGEPLAN YEARS, BUT HE CAPTURED SOME IMPORTANT TEXAS CONCERTS THAT DEPICT A HOMEGROWN BOY LIGHTING UP THE CROWDS WHO LOVED HIM THE MOST.

ROCK PHOTOGRAPHER JOE GIRON TRAVELED ABROAD TO CATCH DIME AND THE BOYS ON THEIR INTERNATIONAL TOURS, INCLUDING THE MONSTERS OF ROCK CONCERT IN MOSCOW.

"IN THE SUMMER OF 2006, VINNIE PAUL DECIDED IT WAS TIME TO BECOME PART OF A BAND AGAIN. HE HELPED FORM HELLYEAH ALONG WITH JERRY MONTANO, TOM MAXWELL, CHAD GRAY, AND GREGG TRIBBETT. LATER, WHEN THE BAND WENT ON THE ROAD, BOB ZILLA BECAME THEIR BASS PLAYER. HEAVY METAL HAD BEEN VINNIE'S LIFE FOR OVER 20 YEARS, AND SO THE MUSIC CALLED HIM HOME. HE KNEW BROTHER DIME WOULD HAVE WANTED IT THAT WAY. SOMEWHERE TONIGHT IN THE HEART OF AMERICA, VINNIE IS ON STAGE LEADING THE ROARING CROWD IN A CHANT ON BEHALF OF HIS BROTHER— "DIMEBAG, DIMEBAG, DIMEBAG . . . ."

In His Words
Tom Maxwell on Dimebag Darrell

VINNIE PAUL   JERRY MONTANO   CHAD GRAY   GREG TRIBBETT   TOM MAXWELL

Waiting for his next show in the upper balcony of the Chicago House of Blues, Tom "Tomcat" Maxwell, currently a member of Hellyeah, looks every bit the metal musician with his black garb and tattoo-covered arms. Yet he is as insightful and articulate as a music historian as he speaks with authority about the impact that Dimebag Darrell had on heavy metal.

"... he was the **MOST IMPORTANT GUITAR PLAYER** of our generation ...anybody can play lead but not anybody can do **SOLOS THAT REACH YOU** ... he was a prodigy ... he was a vehicle between something massive and the guitar he was playing, so **BRUTAL** and **HARDCORE** but **FLAWLESS**. Listen to every band that is out there today ... He was one of the major ingredients that influenced everything you're hearing today. He catered to everyone, but mainly **BLUE-COLLAR AMERICA,** which **NEEDED A CHAMPION** in music at a time in the 1990s when grunge and some real spirit-killing music were out there. There's nothing wrong with that kind of music, but you don't have to look at your toes all the time. Instead, let's have fun and get some aggression out through the music ... Dime made you feel strength—and **EMPOWERED.**"

DISCOGRAPHY

DIME ON DISC

Metal Magic, 1983

Projects in the Jungle, 1984

I Am the Night, 1985

Power Metal, 1988

Cowboys from Hell, 1990

Vulgar Display of Power, 1992

Far Beyond Driven, 1994

The Great Southern Trendkill, 1996

Official Live: 101 Proof, 1997

Reinventing the Steel, 2000

New Found Power, 2004

Rebel Meets Rebel, 2006

DIME ON VIDEO

Dimevision, Vol. 1:
That's the Fun I Have, 2006

THIS COLLECTION OF DARRELL'S PERSONAL VIDEOS FEATURE HIS
FRIENDS AND FAMILY OVER THE YEARS. A GLIMPSE INTO DIME'S
PERSONAL LIFE, THESE HOME MOVIES REVEAL HIS SENSE OF HUMOR
AND HIS UNIQUE PERSPECTIVE—LITERALLY AND FIGURATIVELY—
ON THE WORLD.

DIME GOES TO THE MOVIES

DIME PLAYED AN INSTRUMENTAL TITLED "DIME GOES TO THE
MOVIES," ABBREVIATED AS "D*G*T*T*M," ON THE ALBUM *I AM THE
NIGHT*. LITTLE DID HE KNOW THAT IN THE COMING YEARS, HIS MUSIC
WOULD BECOME PART OF THE SOUNDTRACKS FOR A VARIETY OF FILMS.
THESE RANGE FROM A FORGOTTEN LITTLE B-HORROR DISASTER
CALLED *ZOMBIE NIGHTMARE* TO THE POPULAR JACKIE CHAN ACTION
FLICK *SUPERCOP*.

"Midnite Man" for *Zombie Nightmare,*
1986

"The Badge" for *The Crow,*
1994

"Cemetery Gates" for the "Demon Knight"
episode of *Tales from the Crypt,*
1995

"Strength Beyond Strength" for *Venin Mortel,*
1996

"Caged in a Rage," a solo by Dime for *Supercop,*
1996

"Cat Scratch Fever" for *Detroit Rock City,*
1999

"Immortally Insane" for *Heavy Metal 2000,*
2000

"Avoid the Light" for *Dracula 2000,*
2000

PHOTO CREDITS

All photos and memorabilia provided by the Estate of Darrell Abbott except as noted below. Every reasonable effort has been made to secure permission for the materials in this book. If any acknowledgment has been omitted, please contact the Estate of Darrell Abbott.

Front Cover: **CHAD LEE.**
Back Cover: **MAURO ALVAREZ.**
Table of Contents: **STUART TAYLOR.**

JOE GIRON: 3, 9, 10, 27 bottom, 28, 35, 36 middle, 41, 53, 56, 65 bottom, 66 top right, 78, 80, 83, 86, 88, 89, 91, 92 top, 119, 130 top right, 131 top right, 146 middle, 147 top right, 155, 183 bottom, 186.

CHAD LEE: 1, 2, 4, 6, 7, 116 right, 117, 123 bottom, 128 top and middle, 131 left and bottom, 132 middle, 133, 136, 137, 138, 140, 141, 144 center, 145 bottom, 146 bottom, 147 middle, 150 top and middle, 152, 153 center and bottom, 156, 157, 158 top left, 162, 163, 165, 166, 167, 170, 172 middle left, 173, 175 top and middle, 176 bottom, 177 top, 178 bottom, 179, 180, 181, 182 bottom, 187.

STUART TAYLOR: 8, 11, 34, 38 right, 39 right, 43 top, 46 middle and bottom, 47, 48 bottom, 49 bottom, 54, 55 top and right, 57, 58, 59, 64, 67, 70, 71, 74 center, 76, 77, 79, 84, 96, 101, 116 top left and bottom left, 132 left and right, 135, 151 bottom, 182 top.

MAURO ALVAREZ: 5, 127, 139, 153 top left, 158 top right, 172 top right, 174, 175 bottom, 183 middle, 184 top, 185.

TIFFANY MOORE: 37 top and right, 40 top left, 43 bottom, 44 bottom left and bottom right.

MATTHEW SALACUSE: 97, 183 top.

SUSAN DOLL & DAVID MORROW: 27 top, 65 top and middle, 104 top and left, 105 top and middle, 108, 109, 161 top, 164 top right, middle right, and bottom.

Dug Pinnick photo, 72: Courtesy of **DUG PINNICK**
Kid Rock photo, 73: Courtesy of **KID ROCK**
Hard Rock Vault photos, 129: Courtesy of **DON BERNSTEIN**
106 bottom, 177 middle & bottom: Courtesy of **VIDEO BOB MOSELEY**

ADDITIONAL COPYRIGHT INFORMATION

Damageplan: New Found Power ©2004 Electra Entertainment Group.

Dimebag Darrell's Riffer Madness by Dimebag Darrell Abbott and Nick Bowcott, Alfred Publishing Co., © 2003.

Guitar World © Future Network USA, Future pic.

Guitar Player © Music Player Network.

Pantera: Cowboys from Hell © 1990 Atco Records, Division of Atlantic Recording Corporation.

Pantera: Vulgar Display of Power © 1992 Atco Records, Division of Atlantic Recording Corporation.

Pantera: Far Beyond Driven © 1994 Atlantic Recording Corporation.

Pantera: The Great Southern Trendkill © 1996 Atlantic Recording Corporation.

Pantera: Official Live 101 Proof © 1997 Eastwest Records America.

Pantera: Reinventing the Steel © 2000 Electra Entertainment Group.

Rebel Meets Rebel © 2006 Big Vin Records.

Revolver © Future USA.